"Choose to Climb"
Reaching Your Personal Summit

A Reference Manual For Life's Challenges
With 100 Inspirational Passages Of Clarity, Strategy
And Direction.

By Geraldine Mair

Grosvenor House
Publishing Limited

This book is published by
Grosvenor House Publishing Ltd
Link House
140 The Broadway, Tolworth, Surrey, KT6 7HT.
www.grosvenorhousepublishing.co.uk

A CIP record for this book
is available from the British Library

ISBN 978-1-78623-998-3

This book is dedicated to the two people who hold my heart and that have come into my life and given me unconditional love ever since.

My husband of 28 years Derek, my rock, my best friend and the love of my life, whose constant encouragement, help and belief in me pushed me through doubt to incredible heights.

His insight, inspiration, learning's and drive have been the catalyst that has created the foundation to help me reach my true potential and bring this book to life.

To our son Christopher whose very spirit, compassion and love for all living things, has made us realise everyday how blessed we truly are to have been given such a reward in our lives and who continues to make us incredibly proud, through all his endeavours.

My greatest gift by far has been the privilege of being his mum every single day of his life and for that I have immense gratitude.

We are incredibly proud of the beautiful, loving young man he has become and to whom we wish many adventures in his life's journey and to always remember to help those he meets along the way.

You have our whole heart. You always have.

Love Mum and Dad

This book's title came about from a story that my husband shared with me over seven years ago. After training to be a business coach, Derek was inspired to write a blog that was influenced by a business and financial mentor, the subject matter was on following your passion despite the risks.

In Switzerland there is a range of Alpine mountains and the sixth largest is the Breithorn. Many have succeeded in reaching its summit, however, a good number have lost their life on this and neighbouring peaks, in the pursuit of this aim. The blog is centred on climbing this mountain, and referenced as a metaphor to scale your challenges in life.

At the foot of the mountain is a village called Zermatt, and there in a small graveyard where some of the souls who failed to reach the summit have been laid to rest? This is not a place of sorrow or defeat but one of quiet confidence and power. One headstone of a young male climber only 17 years of age captures this energy best and reads…

"I Chose to Climb".

When I heard this I said to my husband it would be a great name for a book as you can choose to climb in all areas of your life. It was only a passing comment back then, however, when I decided to write this book that story came back into my mind and due to the content, I knew then it could have no other name. I give thanks for all those who dedicated their lives in the pursuit of their dreams and especially to the young man whose sacrifice has become his legacy and the catalyst for the title of this manuscript.

I hope that many others who read this story will develop the courage to ascend their own mountain, instead of ambling at the foot of the hills where no progress can ever be made, so regardless of the outcome or what lies ahead in the pursuit of individual excellence make this the beginning of your new story and ………*"Choose To Climb"*

View the Blog and other learning materials on **www.choosetoclimb.com**

Foreword

by Derek Mair

The passages in this book of life written by my beautiful wife and I mean beautiful in every sense of the word, will allow you to manifest positive changes whenever you are faced with a challenge. Each passage represents a journey of enlightenment and self-discovery, reflecting events that you can each relate to, and for some may be a mirror of where your reality exists today.

As a transformational coach, I have helped hundreds of business owners, leaders and people within many careers realise their potential and push beyond the boundaries of what they believed was possible to achieve in their lives. My organisation has coached many teenagers and adults through confidence and emotional intelligence workshops and I am convinced this book speaks about so many situational events in life that it will become a constant companion to many.

The passages, quotes, affirmations and strategies may allow you to look at your current reality from a different perspective and let you tap into the greatest power at your disposal as human beings; your mind, and through it your ability to 'CHOOSE' and create your destiny.

The fact is that most of you have been raised to accept an ordinary existence. I am not knocking ordinary, I just think that extraordinary is so much better. Perhaps it's not in the search that you find what you have been looking for, it's been inside you all this time; you've just been living with an ordinary consciousness and blind to it.

So how do you get to extraordinary? ...As Gandhi intimates in his famous quote... 'You must'... "Be the change that you wish to see in the World".

Your reality is made up of collective beliefs, determined predominately by emotional perceptions or learned habits through all your life's experiences and events thus far. Your subconscious does not create perceptions but accepts as true those that the conscious mind 'feels' to be true and your reality is consequently formed. Therefore, through your power to question your perception, when you imagine and feel *you* as a better *you* it gives the freedom to create a new extraordinary reality. This is the creation process.

To best apply the passages in this book you must be willing to dream big, and dare to believe that you can overcome the specific effects in your life that are holding you back. Start your journey of self-discovery as Geraldine and I did many years ago, learning to let go of all those limiting beliefs that held us back by developing an extraordinary consciousness. We gracefully accept that we will always be a work in progress, yet happily fulfilled because we choose to climb. Many summits reached many more to come.

Understand everything that now exists was once imagined, therefore imagine often, focusing on how you will feel when you have achieved your goal or dream. Use the heartfelt passages within to bring you back to the experience, joy and gratitude of the present moment, otherwise life will just pass you by. Remember it's not about the destination, it's about the person you become through living the journey and experiencing it to the full, which of course you can only ever do with intention, and in the moment. After all, this thing you call *TIME* is simply a figment of your imagination projected into what you call the future, and a fragmented internal memory recollection system for what you experienced in previous present moments, which you call the past. You are only ever alive and conscious in the present moment... So, get busy living.

Embrace the journey and choose to climb because there is no finish line. Take actions on the strategies within this book to reach an extraordinary consciousness, and a life of fulfilment.

> *"The more you strive for self-actualisation the more you will miss it... The more you learn to be a better you so that you can give more or be of better service to others; your team, customers, community, family and friends, or to a passionate cause, the more you will actualise yourself."*

Derek Mair

Introduction

Many people I have met in life and through my work have challenges and issues as we all do, through engaging with each of them at a personal level they have in their entirety became the inspiration that drove me to put pen to paper and write this book, I will be forever grateful to them all.

My wish for you is that you will visit it often, daily for inspiration and encouragement as you enter your day, or now and again when you feel challenged by life or are struggling and unable to find an answer. Inside the pages of this book lies as array of topics designed to help you with every test you may come across in life and how to conquer them.

Several of the passages address the same subject matter to give you numerous options to deal with a specific challenge in your life, also offering diverse perspectives and different strategies that you can implement over time. The words contain inspiration and a glimpse of your inner resonance that is already a part of you. When you absorb their meanings, they will equip you with strength enabling you to discover a positive attitude within them all.

Invest the time in yourself and it will enable you to see a different way to approach things, on the left-hand page, absorb the messages therein and carry them with you into your days. On the right-hand page is an associated quote, affirmation and strategy in support of the passage, use these as a guide to take action on one that has inspired you.

Knowledge can be a powerful tool, but it is of no value unless you apply that information, when you read this book be open to the learning's within it and be prepared to change your mind.

This action alone can change your life, giving you the impetuous to alter its course. You will never be the same again so...... Choose to Climb!

With all my Love and Gratitude,

Geraldine

Log onto **www.choosetoclimb.com** for a guide to using Affirmations

Table of Contents

"There will be many times in life that you will come across obstacles on your journey, these will come in various guises, people, challenges, events and trials, in the end you can either allow them to block your path or you can climb over or around them and build a new one. Take the chance and see the potential in trying."

Geraldine Mair

1. Applying Knowledge Learned

As you grow and mature it is so important to take responsibility for your actions. Everything that you have learned thus far has laid the foundation for where you are today, and it is only by continuing to learn more about yourself that you can create the platform for a fantastic life.

Although knowledge is a great vehicle, it can only really alter your path by the application of what you have learned. If you never take the steps required with inspired action this can stop you from responding to the call of your life and your purpose. *YOU* are responsible for your decisions and for all your thoughts that manifest through your self-talk, the things that you tell yourself every single day.

Anyone that became exceptional at anything was once where you are now, at the beginning of this journey. So, if you are ready to embrace the challenge and constantly grow to reach new heights, it's going to take effort and commitment on your part and there is no fast fix, you're not going to get there by taking any shortcuts so don't go looking for one, you will have to climb the stairs to reach the top.

Learning can be fun when you select topics that interest or inspire your soul; but there are many ways that you can find out new and innovative things, often it will be listening to others and their own discoveries, that could well lead to the spark that causes you to want to do the same. When you pay attention to what is happening around you the potential to learn something new is assured.

Don't be scared to try different experiences, let the fear that you feel for anything beyond your comfort zone, become the catalyst that creates a juncture to allow the change to begin, your learning is now a wealth of information that resides inside of you and the beauty of this is that it will stay with you now for the rest of your life, it becomes a special treasure that you can never lose... *Choose to Climb.*

Quote

"True knowledge does not come from what you have learned; it comes from applying what you have learned."

Derek Mair

Affirmation

Today I open my mind to learn new things especially about myself. I accept that those opportunities are everywhere, and I choose to boldly act on what I have learned in the knowledge that the experience I gain will make me a better person.

Strategy

When you learn something new from reading this book or through anything in life, act immediately to implement it. It's where learning truly begins and will create a whole new experience that will influence your beliefs and make *you* a stronger version of yourself.

1. Keep a review log highlighting key learning in the pages of the book, this will enable you to reference at a glance the parts that resonate with you the deepest.
2. Create an action plan as it applies to you, and do it.
3. Keep a WIN LOG of actions you have taken and reflect on it often, this will become the fuel that will continually motivate you.

2. A Life of Gratitude

When you awake each day remember life is short so make the very most of every moment that you are here and begin everyone with an attitude of gratitude. You are so blessed and have so much to be thankful for, it's the simplest of things that you take for granted that make your lives comfortable. A tap with running water, a roof over your heads, a warm bed, food on your table, a loving partner, the list goes on.

You become complacent when you cease to notice all the blessings that have already shown up in your experience, living in a culture that is notoriously bad for promoting material gains and striving for more, this can never fill the hole you perceive to be the cause of your misery.

Your riches lie inside of you and not in anything that you can attain, take some time each day to breathe in all the wonder of life so it can take root inside. You develop your character and create memories that you leave for all those whose lives you have touched, when you are no longer physically here. The decisions you make now will cement your future and the road that stretches out in front of you. When you walk in faith and anticipation for what that will bring, you unconsciously give the universe the opportunity to send you more.

When trouble comes into your life and it will, your resolve can be tested but it can also grow your spirit to equip you with the essential tools to push harder through the pain to the rainbow on the other side. When the day is finished be done with it, no matter what it brought, it's in the past and you can no longer affect it, replaying that tune over and over in your mind only amplifies its hold and keeps you stuck. If doubts crept in forget them, tomorrow can be the start of a different chapter, embrace it and begin it well with thanks, another one awaits you to make that difference and give your contribution, rise with the conviction of making it your goal. *Choose to Climb*.

4

Quote

"Begin each day with an attitude of gratitude giving thanks for all that is ahead, know that with every step you take your ability to accomplish greater things than your present position becomes a possibility."

Geraldine Mair

Affirmation

I can see everything around me as miraculous and with this understanding it helps me to embrace all that I have had, all that I have, and all that I will have in the future. With this knowledge I create an attitude of gratitude that brings more good into my life.

Strategy

Every night at the dinner table my family ask these three questions, try them with your family:

- What are you letting go of from today?
- What was your biggest win from today?
- What are you most grateful for from today?

Once you learn to embrace the moment that you are in right now and understand that it is all you can truly affect, you will learn through development of your own thoughts that specific actions which serve you and others for the greater good, lead to true gratitude, and an opportunity for real growth and change.

Developing an attitude of gratitude takes time like it does to build something wonderful, but if you can make it consistent throughout your day it truly has the potential to change your focus and give you the chance to lead a much more inspired life.

3. Never Give Up

Life can test you in ways you never thought it could, it will throw curveballs at you that you didn't see coming, it will attempt to break your very spirit and just when you think you're turning a corner it can knock you right back into the gutter.

Fear is almost always without merit, you create scenarios inside your own thoughts that hardly ever become your reality, yet you give so much energy into frightening yourself with it. Don't be tempted to give up or give in; don't let anything that your limiting beliefs have conjured up in your head control you. You owe it yourself to be free of it. Confront your worries and turn them into the building blocks that will help you to advance forward.

Most people never see their dreams realised because they give up too soon, just when they are on the precipice of success they fail because they could not see what was just around the corner, for them they lacked the faith to believe they could reach it. It is during the challenging times in your life that it is most important to persevere.

On reflection, you will realise that it is when you are most tested, you grow, and why you must realise now the importance of disappointment in the pursuit of success. Sometimes it takes many tries to see an option of a different path that brings you to the place that you were searching for.

Fully armed with this knowledge you then understand this moment of disappointment or difficulty shall pass. Your own experiences can offer you the information required to help others, if they too find themselves in a place of struggle.

Choose to *Get Up! Step Up and Never Give Up!* You become a winner when you refuse to yield, so never stay miserable and remember why you started, live your life with gratitude without limits...and *Choose to Climb*.

Quote

"Never give up believing for a better tomorrow, every day is an opportunity to change your story."

Geraldine Mair

Affirmation

When I commit to action I see it through to its end. An obstacle is simply an opportunity in disguise that I am equipped to conquer. Whenever I feel defeated by an experience, I will not let it define me. I will get up, step up and never give up. I am proud of myself for even daring to try and I grow in strength with every forward step I take.

Strategy

1. Define exactly what you want to achieve.
2. Define WHY you want to achieve it and write it down.
3. Take at least 10 minutes every day to visualise what you will feel when experiencing your *WHY's* (when you're emotional 'why's' are strong enough you will be surprised at the differences that will materialise in your life).
4. Break down what you want to achieve into smaller steps and create a plan.
5. Commit at the start of each day to take some small action that day.
6. Ensure your confidence comes from a platform of trying your very best to achieve what you want, and focus on your *WHY's*.
7. When things are not going so well, don't beat yourself up, repeat steps three to six more often during the day.

4. Priceless Diamonds

People spend so much time looking for recognition from others and define their worth based on that external input. It is so important to love yourself first, be true to who you really are, set your standards and make it non-negotiable how you allow others to treat you.

Never doubt yourself, have the courage to trust what you are capable of. Remember even when you think there is no one else, there will always be one person that has the capacity to love and believe. That person *IS* you! You need to become your best supporter first; this ultimately sets the standard that everything else will be defined by.

You all have a purpose and it can take a lifetime to really discover what that is, but one thing is certain, the way that you make others feel will be the measure of that legacy and what they will remember.

True wealth cannot be measured in monetary gain or in the titles that are given for academic achievement, the true value lies in the individual contributions that we make to one another, and it can start today with you. Everything in life is cyclical, you experience that which you are in your reality; you will always get back what you put out.

You are a miraculous creation of which the likes will never pass through here again; caterpillars turn into butterflies, as sand turns into pearls. All things that are worth their weight in gold take time to mould and you are no different in the creation process.

Look within and love deeply everything that is you, never think of yourself as lessor or lower in value than another person, you may believe you are nothing more than a rough-cut stone, but polish it up and you will find the true essence just below the surface, a priceless diamond... *Choose to Climb*.

Quote

"How powerful and brilliant you were born is only limited by your belief in how powerful and brilliant you are."

Derek Mair

Affirmation

I am a unique individual and I choose to celebrate my differences. "I am filled with light, love and peace and I treat myself with kindness and respect. I don't have to be perfect; I just have to be me and I give myself permission to shine. I love who I am and will embrace the qualities in each person that I meet today.

Strategy

1. Keep a daily Win Log.
2. Record at least one Win regardless of how small it is everyday – Look back on your win log each week and praise yourself.
3. Create a mental picture of your *ideal* self.
4. Your *ideal* self is the person you would like to become; how you would act and behave if you believed you had the choice to do so.
5. Act like that person *NOW* (because it is your true self).

5. Find Your Greatness Within

Are you choosing your life path out of convenience, availability or what you think others want you to do, this happens when you operate from an internal belief pattern that coerces you to think, you are unable of achieving your own goals and dreams, or, that you are unworthy of that level of success due to a programmed fear within you.

It seems almost ridiculous to expect something that amazing so you never give any energy or thought to that vision. There are no guarantees in this life but one thing is for sure, if you never try there can be no result. Just imagine for a moment if you will, being good at something you don't really like doing, which is where a lot of people are in relation to their jobs. How amazing and fantastic could you be doing something that you love?

Don't be afraid to try or to fail, it teaches you strength and how to overcome your personal challenges. Life's trials are not unique to you; they happen to everyone in differing degrees and help develop your mental tolerance and a strong character giving you the tools to help others to avoid the pitfalls. When you do not achieve the conclusion that you aimed for in a project or task, you often look on it as a defeat. This thought process can keep you stuck in a position of stalemate and prevent real progress because you give up. Never look at this experience as something bad, trying and failing is progress in every sense of the word. It can prove to be the vehicle that really catapults you forward with renewed vigour and a desire to try again.

Once you come to understand that your decisions in this life ultimately create your own reality, it will be in the implementation of this awareness that you will become all that you want to be. Transformation can happen in a moment, it only takes a change of mind and a will to follow a better path, in doing so you can tip the scales in your favour towards a more fulfilling journey. Learn to walk by faith and not by sight, get out onto your ledge and make the jump and grow your wings on the way down, your future is waiting for you to embrace your brilliance and find the greatness that lies within... *Choose to Climb.*

Quote

"You will never succeed greatly unless you are willing to fail greatly."

Derek Mair

Affirmation

I can become all that I believe that I can. Today I give myself permission to step into my greatness and follow my true path. I know I am capable, I deserve it and I commit to become all that I want to be, do and have in this life.

Strategy

Do not entertain people, or your own inner voice, that reinforces belief patterns that have kept you in the same place for years. If you don't start today then five years from now you will still be on that merry-go-round on the road to nowhere. Look for the greatness that is already within you.

1. Ask yourself when do I feel most important or fulfilled? Whatever you are doing when you feel this way is what you are meant to do.
2. Set a goal to pursue what makes you feel satisfied either through your career or hobby.
3. Imagine how you will feel when you are doing it as often as possible.
4. Embrace the potential for failure as your greatest opportunity to learn and if you hit the wall repeat step three and climb over or around it.

6. Remembering To Take Notice

Every day you can get so caught up in all the daily tasks and things you must do, that you forget to pay attention to the people around you. Forgetting to nurture your relationships because you become complacent and believe they will always be there for you regardless of your own behaviours. If you constantly have your face in a phone or computer when someone is trying to talk to you or carve out quality time, don't be surprised if they tire of trying to get your attention, or worse replace you with someone that will.

An easy and obvious way to show love is to give consideration, though some people behave like it's a lot harder than it sounds. All of you are getting caught up in this technological age, and the temptation to remain that way overtakes everything else. Be aware of what you are doing, attention and awareness is the cornerstone and foundation that you build your love and relationships upon. What you appreciate grows and flourishes what you ignore withers and dies, so make it a priority to teach each other to participate in real social interaction, encouraging quality time away from distractions. Be attentive today to your wife, husband, partner and your children who seek nothing more than your unconditional love.

The only way to ensure a bright and happy future is to build one that is based on communication and understanding. Creating a balance that does not require you to give up on what you view as urgent, whilst making it non-negotiable with yourself to invest time in those things that are truly important. Choose to lead your life by example and notice the beauty that you are a part of everyday, live your life to your fullest potential and never give up on your dreams. Spending time together in connection is worth more than any task, don't show anger at interruption, show patience and love. People are more important than anything else, life and love can be fragile, nurture them and the rewards are limitless...
Choose to Climb.

Quote

"There is beauty in all of life and nature but unfortunately not everyone takes the time to really see it. Make time for love, and love will make time for you."

Geraldine Mair

Affirmation

Today I make time to show love and appreciation to those special people in my life. I deserve to be loved and I allow myself this gift. I am ready for a healthy, loving relationship and I am the perfect partner for my ideal match.

Strategy

Be the one who causes the change, be the one who others will choose to emulate. See the gift in everyday that you are given. Take time to invest in those around you who need your attention. Make it non-negotiable, life is short but all the best things in life are truly free. Love, kindness, giving, compassion and gratitude, and they always deliver the greatest results:

1. Decide on a date night with your partner and pencil it into your respective diaries.
2. Each of you write on a small piece of paper in one sentence, six dates each of you would like to go on with each other on your date night, making 12 in total, one for every month. Fold them and put them in a jar mixing, them up without sharing with each other.
3. Pick a night to reveal your date for that week.

Devote at least 60 minutes unreserved time to your kids each day doing whatever they are doing or want to do.

7. The Power of Drive, Determination and Dedication

To achieve any kind of personal or professional success in this life, you must be prepared to do what no one else will. You will need to have an unwavering work ethic, be prepared to go that extra mile, to stand out, and invest the time when others won't.

It is truly amazing that some can find every excuse in the world for themselves, yet identify the shortcomings in those around them, they fail to recognise that the world within them is the only one that can be influenced or changed. This is where the real transformation begins. You cannot stand in judgement of anyone else without first looking at improving yourself. Personal development can open many doors and help you to view challenges and events in a completely different way and with a much more constructive response.

Grow into a person who refuses to look down at others to raise themselves higher, this unethical approach does not work and achieves no real satisfactory outcome. The price you will need to pay for reaching your own personal success summit will be your dedication and focus on self-improvement, through a disciplined mind and a willing heart.

Never doubt, never hesitate, and never question that which you believe to be true in your own heart. Engaging with this kind of unwavering faith and enthusiasm will take you places that right now you can only dream of. Under no circumstances cease to improve your own self-limiting conditioning to drive yourself towards completing your aims and desires. In doing so your dreams will no longer be a figment of your imagination they will become your reality.

The true wealth of anyone is not what they hold in their hands but what they feel in their hearts and show to the world every day. Seek such similar people out in life, learn from them, emulate them and make a conscious choice to live without any limit, choose always to climb higher, and always with a grateful heart... *Choose to Climb.*

Quote

"There are two great pains you will suffer in life, discipline or regret, one brings results in the now, the other torment in the future... You always have a choice which one to pick."

Derek Mair

Affirmation

I can achieve all the goals that I set out for myself. I understand that success lies on the other side of failure. I will create my own life and I have the determination and drive to accomplish all that I seek. Today I follow my heart and discover my destiny, I am meant to do great things and know that I am limited only by my vision of what is possible.

Strategy

Remember that when you have a drive to achieve anything that is emotionally important to you, and attach enough emotional energy to that desire, you create a forward momentum that becomes hard to stop.

1. Split a sheet of paper into three columns. At the top of each column write the words from left to right HOW? WHAT? WHY?
2. In the middle WHAT? column write specifically the goal you want to achieve in the present tense with a date, e.g. I am a non-smoker on Aug xx xxxx.
3. In the right hand, WHY? column write at least 20 deep emotional whys? you want to achieve your goal.
4. In the left hand, HOW? column write a series of actions you are going to take to achieve your goals and experience your Whys.
5. Read and visualise experiencing your Whys every morning after you awake.

8. The Power of Forgiveness

There is weakness and faults in us all; you are human and susceptible to these traits. When you are offended or hurt by another person's actions, it can be very difficult to see beyond the offence so you replay it over and over in your mind, which causes distress through over analysis of your own or another person's behaviours.

If you have a strong character you can often see beyond the faults of others and forgive them their follies, if you are weaker you will find it challenging to do so and may even elect to end friendships and relationships, instead of forgiving a perceived wrong that has been done to you.

When you learn to forgive others, it will set you free from pain, hurt or anger, and you'll discover that taking ownership for someone else's behaviours can only hold power over you if you 'choose' to let it.

There are so many people that are afraid to forgive; they want to remember the hurt they felt so they feel justified in the choice to isolate that individual or as a reason to use the information to gossip to others. This interaction gives them the fuel and encouragement that supports their choices and keeps them on this destructive path. You need to realise that there is another way. True forgiveness releases you from emotive *AND* immobilising strongholds, and expands your awareness of others. It helps to develop emotional intelligence, creating a platform to view situations, events and communications from other perspectives, so you can work through any situation far more effectively.

Throughout your life there will always be those who challenge your boundaries, or violate your values, how you choose to respond is the key to mature growth. Take control and stop allowing these situations to fester and damage your life; do not allow the actions of another to ruin every new day and all your tomorrows. You ultimately choose your own mood so let it go or let them go... It's the fastest way to rid your life of emotions that don't serve your higher good... *Choose to Climb.*

Quote

"True Forgiveness prevents YOU from being chained to other people's behaviours in YOUR past, and without excusing those behaviours, releases YOU to focus your energy on that which enriches YOUR future."

Derek Mair

Affirmation

Today I will choose to see things from another's perspective. I refuse to jump to conclusions without seeking to understand before being understood. I offer and ask for forgiveness for all the wrongs that have been done to me or that I have done to others in my past, I release them and all the associated emotions. I am filled with light, love and peace and choose to respond, and not react to events in my life.

Strategy

Put Yourself Back in Control:

- Forgiveness is strength, an emotional muscle that you can develop. Choosing to address any wrong from this angle places the control firmly in your hands. This does not mean that you are necessarily ok with a specific treatment that someone projected. You should be assertive in pointing out to the offender how it made you feel, holding them accountable for their behaviour.
- When you reach the decision to allow it to leave your consciousness it simply means you have decided that it's no longer worth the constant anguish and worry that can arise from these feelings. You can still make a mindful choice to forgive that person whether they are aware of it or not, refusing to allow it any negative energy gives yourself the gift to be able to detach from it.

17

9. How Much Do You Want a Fulfilling Life?

You are the creator of your life; every day you make choices that have the power to alter all your tomorrows. Don't think about what you're going to be doing a week from now, a month from now, a year from now. What you do today and the action that you set in motion will alter all those outcomes in the future. Therefore, if you're not achieving your aims you need to change the way you think *now!*

If you are worried every day, anxious about your future and constantly complaining about what you don't have, you are creating a life that will guarantee you a whole lot more of the same; what you say you don't want.

However, on the flip side of this is a change in perspective. See opportunities not hurdles, see love not hate, see peace not conflict, you have everything you need inside you right now to make better decisions that will guarantee a better outcome.

To become the very best version of yourself you must step away from what society expects from you and spend time in development of your own dreams. You are all capable of so much, yet you leave an enormous amount of talent on the table because you listened to those people who put you down or doubted your abilities, and then chose to buy into those lies.

I believe that there is always a day of reckoning and there is a science behind the energy that you emit into the space around you. Making the decision to aim for the greater good, in all you set out to do for yourself and others, is by far the healthiest choice. Understand that every selection you make adds to the strength or weakness of your spirit and has the power to be eternal. Don't try to find a purpose, follow your passion and make your lifetime matter. Better questions lead to better decisions, which ultimately lead to better outcomes and this will guarantee you the best opportunity to have a rewarding life. Believe in yourself and the endless power of possibility... *Choose to Climb.*

Quote

"Life is not about finding a purpose to create happiness; it's about being happy and following your passion to discover a wonderful sense of fulfilment and an evolving sense of purpose along the journey."

Derek Mair

Affirmation

I am the creator of my own life; my unique skills and talents can make a profound difference in this world. Today I follow my heart to discover my destiny, I choose to realise my full potential knowing that my life purpose can be whatever I choose to make it, and I do choose to make it...

Strategy

1. Reflect upon what it is that you do, that when you do it, you feel in the moment a total sense of fulfilment and enjoyment
2. Decide exactly where you want to be in 90 days' time along your journey (make it realistic).
3. Write it down as a goal on the back of a business card and keep it on your person reading it as many times as possible during the day
4. See yourself in your mind's eye achieving your goal and how you will feel about yourself as you achieve it.
5. Start each new day by writing down just one small action that will move you towards this goal.
6. Take inspired action by doing your one thing before you do anything else that day, if possible.
7. Make this a daily habit and before long this will become your normality and your life will be one of accomplishment.

10. Attention Seekers

Do you have a constant need for everything to be about you? Do you court an insatiable desire to be liked by every Tom, Dick, and Harry? Understand this is simply a reflection of your own sense of self-worth... You must reach a point in your life where you are sufficient and intrinsically know this without any external validation. Recognise you are coming from a place of lack that was conditioned into you, probably unconsciously, by one of your early influencers.

Confidence through loving yourself for who you are attracts attention, people gravitate towards these individuals. In contrast desperation and neediness repels and no one wants to listen to a person who spends that much time talking about their woes, it's just exhausting and draining to be around.

There is no need to constantly seek the recognition of anyone, be yourself and people will love you for it. The growth of a person is necessary for change to happen, learn to love yourself first, forgive yourself and thank yourself for who you are and you will gain an inner confidence without needing to have it confirmed.

Choose happiness, choose laughter, and choose joy, choose self-love and all the attention you seek will radiate from you like you have been illuminated from within, drawing to you that which you pursue.

Do not follow a quest for perfection, you are already perfectly imperfect. Do not chase the ideal life that you witness in another, everybody has challenges and hurdles, some you will know nothing about. Comparing yourself to them and wishing to have their life is futile and only drives you back to a position of self-lack.

When you love who you are and show that to others, every experience and connection can change your future, rebuilt on life-long relationships that will last the test of time... *Choose to Climb.*

Quote

"Gaining an audience to impress or be the centre of attention is not the same as gaining loving friendships."

Geraldine Mair

Affirmation

I am happy with who I am. I will show my true self to the world with every day that I am gifted to be here. I love myself no matter what and will make it my intention to take an interest in others, knowing that will show the best of me and people will love me because of it. I accept that I am already enough, I always have been.

Strategy

Stay true to who you are. If there are aspects of yourself that you dislike take this as the sign to change then; starting right now. Invest the necessary time to discover your authenticity and celebrate your uniqueness.

Every morning for next 30 days stand in front of a mirror and ask yourself and answer these three questions...

1. [Say your name], I am proud of you for... name seven things... it can be the same seven things each day.
2. [Say your name], I forgive you for... seven things.
3. [Say your name], I commit to you.... seven things.

Note: This strategy is universal and can be applied to many other challenges, as it reprograms the subconscious mind building better internal belief patterns, that with repetition creates the desired response for change.

11. Memories of Loved Ones Lost

There is really no such thing as the permanent death of someone that you have loved. The more focus and attention you give to a memory or a feeling the stronger it can become. It's all about the love that you retain in your heart and the impact they made to your life during their time here.

When you choose to remember, you open your heart and allow all the wonderful memories to live there, not in the cemetery, not in the garden of remembrance, not in other countries if they were buried there, you will find their very essence wherever you are. They are a part of you and beside you every step of the way. People die only when you forget to remember them.

Those who enter and leave your life touch you in ways that can be hard to explain, these are the very special souls that deserve a piece of your heart forever, for you are never the same for having known them. The beauty that you now miss is not in the memory but in the things that you have felt with them and will never forget. Be grateful for the joy of that experience and try not to constrain it through the pain of remembering.

Be kind to others who have felt incredible loss, you will all know this level of pain at some point in your own life and there should never be a time limit placed on it. It's impossible to be the same person that you were, it's more about finding a way forward through the acceptance of that which you cannot change and learn a new way to live. In doing so you will hopefully learn to embrace with a grateful heart everything you have had, what you have now, and what you have still to receive.

Life is challenging and there are many obstacles that will be placed on your path. There have been many others who in the midst of their pain found strength in the participation of positive acts like charities to remember their loved ones, or by helping others that are going through the same torment. This can give hope that your journey ahead can get easier when you become open to it... *Choose to Climb*.

Quote

"Those that we hold the memory of in our hearts, our thoughts and in our words, are never ever lost."

Geraldine Mair

Affirmation

I will cherish all those whom I love every day. I am grateful to have all those who have enriched my life in every moment that I have shared with them. I choose to always remember those who have gone, with love and gratitude for the blessings that they brought to me. I am a better person for having known them and I will be forever enriched through knowing them.

Strategy

Losing people that you love will be the hardest thing you will ever have to do, but it will be a part of all of your lives. There can be no time limit on this emotion and each of you will process it in a different way.

1. Remembering and choosing to honour a special person is a wonderful thing to do and can help us to celebrate their life using a positive response.
2. Give yourself emotional permission to move forward and reach a level of acceptance and peace for that which you can no longer change.
3. Using a sad experience to assist others in the same situation can help you to heal and give you a purpose once more to continue through life, via a different route but with real optimism that you helped another person to gain hope that was lost.
4. Speak to a therapist or join a group that specialises in helping you to process the hurt in a constructive way.

23

12. Beautiful Partnerships

Passion in humans can be very quick to develop. A pretty smile, a sexy dress, a beautiful man with piercing eyes in a very smart suit can catch you off guard. But this can be nothing more than a fleeting moment. Intimacy is something that develops over time at a very deep level of connection.

I often think if people treated each other the way they did in the beginning there would never need to be an end, as both would be trying to keep it fresh and exciting. So many of you miss the things you used to love in your partners because you just don't look anymore, you've become complacent and stale.

When real advanced intimacy is reached in one another you create an unshakable bond, not just on a physical level but a mental and spiritual one too.

If your experiencing difficulties try remembering what you loved in that person, the things that made it necessary for you to have them as your life partner, your best friend, your confidante and if it's not too late, strive to get that back.

The truth is everyone is going to cause you hurt at some point, even if it was unintentional, it's the very nature of being human, but the key is finding someone that you are prepared to accept with all their flaws and love them anyway.

No one is perfect nor should you expect them to be, mistakes and disagreements are normal and natural but deciding to remember all the things that are right instead of the few things that upset you can guarantee a long happy life with your best friend.

Relationships require investments of time and effort, surprises and thoughtful gestures. Start again today, I guarantee your rewards will be amazing when you are grateful for your husband or your wife and I don't just mean some of the more obvious rewards, I mean everything... *Choose to Climb*.

Quote

"Love is the greatest of emotions and gratitude is the great multiplier of love. Remember what you nurture grows, what you ignore dies... Don't give up on anything that you love, work at it and the rewards will be priceless."

Geraldine Mair

Affirmation

Today I will see the beauty in my partner; I will choose to remember all the special gifts and attributes that drew me to them in the beginning. I will be thankful to have them in my life and I will invest the time required to nurture the relationship to ensure its longevity.

Strategy

If you are having difficulty in your relationship, resolve right now, from this moment forward for at least 30 days, to simply give love to your partner. No matter how frustrated or angry you become internally, resolve to externally only show love in return:

1. Giving love will multiply love... so give love like you've never given before.
2. At least at the end of 30 days it will be reciprocated or not, and you will know. Regardless your heart will have grown.

13. Anything is Possible When You Believe in Yourself

The world can be a scary place, sometimes things can and do go wrong or they don't work out the way you had hoped. That's life, and your internal dialog will create fear to hold you back from trying new things or following your desires. If you have a dream in your heart, you must go after it, if you don't then know that you will feel pain in the future; the pain of regret.

You may come across people that will try to discourage you, using negative tactics with only the intention of holding you back... People who are emotional vampires will tell you that you can't get what you want. Forgive them; it is simply their own beliefs that prevent them considering the possibility of a better outcome. They view it as a risk and wish you to do the same.

You have two choices, you can stay, run with the herd, bury your hopes and dreams and conform to the society you think you fit into, or you can separate yourself from negative influencers that no longer serve you, encourage you, or support you. If you want something bad enough then go get it, no matter what it takes.

Don't be afraid to fail or make decisions it's not over till you win; you've just got to keep rising after you fall. Success is just over the hill or around the next corner, so keep on pushing on.

You must believe that something different can happen for you, that you deserve it and you're going to work for it. In the words of Henry Ford, *"The people who continually say they can or they cannot are both usually right."* Choose carefully what side of the fence you're aiming for.

Dig deep, find out what makes you fulfilled, even if it sounds crazy to other people, that wish was placed in your heart for a reason; it's God's gift to you that it's already yours. Decide, make a choice and follow that commitment... *Choose to Climb.*

Quote

"How powerful and brilliant you were born, is only limited by your belief in how powerful and brilliant you are."

Derek Mair

Affirmation

Fear is only a feeling; it cannot hold me back, I know that I can master anything if I do it enough times. Today I am willing to fail to succeed. I'm proud of myself for even daring to try; I put my trust in my inner guidance growing in strength with every step I take. I harness all the power that I have within and I choose to believe that I deserve all the good that is already on its way to me. I am grateful for the opportunity to realise and live my dreams.

Strategy

In simple terms you can rewrite disempowering beliefs that you have formed in your mind through your life experiences thus far:

1. If you can imagine what it will feel like to be you in your dream, then you can break the cords that bind you one step at a time.
2. Listen to the only true voice that matters; your own.
3. Find out about how you think and operate through reading personal development books, attending seminars, or get a coach.
4. Be open to what you learn and start to ask better questions of yourself when you hear a disempowering belief through your inner voice.
5. Talk to yourself and rationalise the emotional signal you are experiencing from this disempowering belief.
6. Replace the limiting belief with a new belief through repetition of action supported by the affirmations and visualisation techniques in this book.

14. Random Acts of Kindness

When you interact with others that you meet daily through random acts of kindness, you create limitless power, and go from being strangers to becoming connected at a human level.

When you make a conscious effort to help those who cross our path, you put yourself into a place of joy, and feel an inner peace that comes from giving without expecting anything in return.

Imagine the impact that you could have on your beautiful planet, if you chose to see everything from a different perspective and without judgement. You would come to realise that you do not know the history of many of those whom you choose to judge; by adopting this attitude you could ensure that a lot more people would be hurting a whole lot less. Opinions of the masses cannot be changed overnight, though one day at a time, one person at a time can indeed be the catalyst for change to commence. Don't look to someone else to start the wheels moving, it begins with you.

Why not distribute all the kindness you can muster, go out daily and reach as many people as you can, smile at a stranger, hold a door open for a mother with a pram and a toddler, allow someone with a couple of items to skip in front of you at the checkout, it's tiny gestures that can change a person's day without you really being aware of how much you added to it. Not only will it have a positive effect on the recipient, it will lift your own day higher than you can imagine. When you choose to give without expectation of receiving, it's a guarantee that what you put out is coming right back to you. It's simply cause and effect in action.

Give gratitude for experiences you receive, enjoy the results that giving creates in the hearts of those you touch and allow them to reciprocate. Keep the wheels of love and gratitude turning in your lives, knowing that in doing so it has the capacity to change the world, I do believe it might just be the only thing that can....
Choose to Climb.

Quote

"I choose to no longer have an outlook that is based on doctrine, dogma, or any kind of bias, I choose to operate from a platform of kindness, this will be my creed."

Geraldine Mair

Affirmation

I will always come from a place of compassion. I will choose to help whenever I can without expectation of any return. I am here to aid not judge. I will choose to step out from the herd when others won't and be the change.

Strategy

Make it your mission to perform at least one random act of kindness each day to a stranger or loved one, and soon you will inherit abundance and joy in your life:

- One small thing each day creates three hundred and sixty-five little offerings to others by the end of each year. There is no joy in entering anything with an attitude of "what's in it for me". Trust me when I tell you, this is the wrong way around, flip the coin over and choose the opposite as listed on the passage, it is in the act of giving that you receive and when you give of yourself often it creates a waterfall of abundance that follows everywhere you go.
- It just starts with one small unselfish act. Not only will the people's day that you helped change for the better, yours will too. Let's start an avalanche of kindness wherever we go. There is too much pain and hurt in the world, you can make a difference and it can start right now. Choose to pay it forward... *Choose to Climb.*

15. A Judgemental Heart

How many people have you met during your lives that were judgemental? It happens way too often, judging people's actions, questioning their intentions, which at times can be shrouded in cruel jibes or comments.

If this is you, understand that you are only suppressing your spirit, at the very least try to be curious before condemning. Imagine what your life could look like if you stopped making unconstructive, judgemental, assumptions about other people that you meet, why not look for the good and respect their personal journey, even when it differs from your own. There is always a different perspective.

If this happens to you realise that your happiness cannot be overshadowed by the limited thinking of another, unless you allow it to be. This is their programming; their characteristics, being expressed through their own belief systems, so don't take ownership of their issues by reacting.

The problem is not you, it never was, you are simply a target, someone to help them to perhaps feel more superior in some way. When you come across this kind of behaviour it stems from a very low sense of self-worth, so they attack others to feel more significant.

There is little that can be done to effectively change a person who believes there is little wrong with their actions towards others, so don't try. They must come to this realisation on their own, though you can refuse to engage with their negative actions. Sadly, their limited thinking would still cause them to find a way to judge you regardless of what you do or say.

That said don't give your power away to another by allowing unacceptable behaviour towards you. Only you control how much events affect you. As Dr Seuss said: *"Be who you are and say how you feel because those who mind don't matter and those who matter don't mind"*.

Choose the path less travelled and lead by example, choose to be with those people who encourage you and lift you higher, they will support and inspire you to follow your true path… *Choose to Climb.*

Quote

"When you resist the urge to judge someone you move from a state of criticism to one of curiosity, enabling you to learn more about the others perspective... Turning your original indifference into perhaps making a difference."

Derek Mair

Affirmation

I am a person who sees the beauty in all life. I will consciously be aware of what I say about others to others. I will place no preconceptions on people that I do not know. I will respect that their life story if different from mine and be more open to acceptance.

Strategy

You are all guilty of engaging with gossip, in your work places, in social circles and in life in general. Start today with a new vision, remember anyone that you perceive to be doing something wrong, simply has a different perspective on life than you. Their upbringing will have been different, their friends and influencers will be different. This does not mean you should judge them you should simply try to understand the alternative approaches that people take, and adjust your views accordingly:

1. If you know someone that has offended you or others on a regular basis, remove yourself from that circle; it's not your job to fix anyone. Spend more time with positive people instead.
2. Lead by example without compromising your own values. Make a choice to get to know individuals without prejudging them.

16. Building a Strong Character

Life has a habit of challenging you when you least expect it. This is the time that your character is put into question. In this moment you must be willing with courage to face your fears head on; there is no point in pretending that nothing has happened, burying your head in the sand and hoping that the next day it will have gone.

If you are suffering through pain, be it a personal loss or a situation in your life that is testing your resolve, the challenge will not wait.

Life does not look back; it is only ever in motion moving constantly forward. Living with a past mentality can never drive you in the direction you seek; it can only keep you in reverse. You can decide to take action, do not let events that have happened in your past define you, it is not you, if you continue to live every day locked in your past and in your pain, you will infect every tomorrow that you are gifted.

The only way you change is to grow through learning to overcome, when you are wounded deeply by traumas in your past in can be hard to get ahead with any degree of certainty, yet there can be little point in directing any energy to that time, in this regard you should not allow it to govern over you today. Self-improvement takes time and should be viewed with a one day at a time approach.

Your character cannot be truly developed during your harmonious times, only when you gain experience through the trials that you face can you emerge strengthened and inspired to achieve more. If something in your past is limiting you, it needs to stay in your past, accept fully what you cannot alter and find a way to control it... Take your love, take your memories, take your hopes and your dreams, and keep on your journey. Your strong character will surface when you defend your boundaries without hesitation and step into your power showing the world that you are fierce... *Choose to Climb.*

Quote

"The power that is evident in each of us is hidden a lot of the time, only rising to the surface when tested; Finding yourself in emotional agony without any longing to yield to those difficulties, that is strength."

Geraldine Mair

Affirmation

I am greater than any challenge that I may face as I was born with the ability to overcome all things. Today I put my full trust in my inner guidance. I know I'll grow in strength with every forward step, I accept my hesitations and shortcomings as part of me and make room for victory because I believe in myself, and that there's nothing I cannot do."

Strategy

When you come across a time in your life that has caused you immense struggle, be it emotional, financial, spiritual or physical. Listen to your heart.

1. Consider the practice of meditation to clear your mind every morning when you awake. It puts you into a state of peace, re-balancing all the bio-chemicals within your body to better prepare for the day ahead.
2. Factor a 30-minute walk into your day, as you walk say your affirmation repeatedly to yourself and observe how your energy improves... Let go of anything that is troubling, or look at it from a different perspective, altering your attitude toward it. You will feel wonderful and want to do it more.
3. Focus on the lesson learnt within every experience, embrace every event in your life as a teacher and come to realise it was necessary for you to experience to move forward.

17. Lasting Friendships

There are many kinds of relationships, and there are different degrees of affection that are shared within them. You can choose the level of love that you are prepared to invest in another person... The best kind though is one that has room to grow and change over time, ripening and deepening in the process.

If there is a deep connection it must be based on both parties being, patient and considerate. There is no room in any union for an inflated ego, a need to be right all the time, or one who constantly belittles or berates the other to make themselves feel superior in some way. Friendships should create bonds that send you on an incredible journey, an adventure, an experience that should not cause pain or hurt.

It's not a requirement for you to collect friendships like possessions. Having an array of contacts doesn't necessarily ensure that you will always be in demand. You will find in time and through personal experience the friends who travel with you on your life's journey are the ones that matter the most, and will make you feel significant and cherished.

When you practice loyalty with others, you come to realise that often the strongest connections were not based on those who gave us advice, but with those caring souls who simply listened, shared our pain and were at our side in moments of despair. Often real friendship requires no words only a presence and a promise not to walk behind or in front, but to walk by our side with a supporting arm creating an imprint on our hearts that is sure to endure the test of time.

Lasting friendship in life can often be measured in the times when you feel you are separated from those whom you love and understanding that no matter how much time passes or how long you are apart nothing has changed.

Quote

"Do not complain if you have no special people in your life to call 'friend'; Become one to someone else and you will never need protest again."

Derek Mair

Affirmation

I am kind to others. I love the people that I care about. I nurture the relationships that I have in my life. I have amazing friends that have expanded my life. I love meeting new people, as it's an opportunity to get to know them and extend the hand of friendship once more.

Strategy

When you are looking to grow your friendship circle the first thing you must do is work on yourself, learning the art of communication is a skill that takes time.

1. The best way to be a good friend is to be a good listener. When you give others a platform to express themselves it grows real trust between all parties involved.
2. Create a non-judgemental forum where everyone can feel safe.
3. Try not to interrupt when others are sharing important information with you, it can't always be about you all the time. There should be equal give and take in all relationships to give them the necessary space to expand and grow.
4. If you find it difficult to interact with others the best place to find new people to meet will be at local clubs, gyms, night classes and networking events. Stepping out of your comfort zone will be scary but not as much us being on your own. Get out there and make it happen, bring your authentic self to the table and the right people who resonate with your values will connect with you allowing friendships to flourish.

18. The Road Less Travelled

The good things in our lives always come to those that are willing to step out from the crowd, follow their dreams, and dare to fail.

It is not cowardice that holds most people back, it is conformity. It is easy to bow to conventionality and use the blame and excuse game, the only problem is that when you follow the crowd you tend to get lost in it.

When you push yourself in areas of your life that you never believed that you could, you develop an inner strength, one that cannot be found unless you have faced real life challenges that lie beyond the acceptance of mediocrity.

People that succeed in anything do not get lowered onto the summit, they climb with everything that they have and they keep going because they know the view at the top will be more than worth the pain of getting there.

Unless you face your most difficult realities and the trials that ultimately push you to act, your chances of reaching your own personal peak will be narrow.

Once the decision has been made that you are no longer willing to settle for anything less than your best, there isn't an obstacle in your way that can stop you... And with the right attitude you've already programmed the coordinates to reach your greatest altitude. With a desire and drive that has a powerful machine at its very core success is surely guaranteed.

When you have the chance to go in a different direction than the one you are currently on, you set in motion a chain reaction. By venturing down the road less travelled it can, and often is, the one that makes the biggest difference. Believe you can, know you deserve the success you are looking for, break down your barriers, listen to your heart, build your staircase and choose to climb.

Quote

"When the road splits at the junction and everyone chooses to go to the right, you will choose the left knowing that whatever it brings, has the potential to make all the difference because you took the chance that so many others wouldn't."

Geraldine Mair

Affirmation

Today I follow my heart and discover my destiny. I am meant to do great things, I am the captain of my ship driving forward from the helm. Today I give myself permission to be greater than my fears. I have a great attitude for success and deserve to have an amazing life. I will be the one who takes the least popular choice and show others there is a better way. I will step away from the pack and leave my mark on the world by the way I live my life.

Strategy

Fear is not real, only danger is real, though both feelings have the same internal electro-chemical reaction on our bodies. When you are faced with an opportunity in your life that induces a sense of fear:

1. Rationalise your emotions by asking yourself is this fear or real danger.
2. Ask yourself what is the worst thing that could possibly happen if I take this opportunity and it does not work out, and can I live with it?
3. Do not be swayed by those who tell you that you can't or that you will fail as they are imposing their own fears onto you.
4. Be strong in your own convictions and abilities to reach your own personal summit.

19. Life Without Limits

Our lives are made up of many opportunities that you can choose to take advantage of, but this sometimes means other doors may close. You always have a different path that you can elect to travel; therefore, I believe there are no confines to the life you can lead.

It should never matter what background you're coming from or where you grew up, for with the right attitude and knowledge through continuous learning about you, all things are possible in this life.

Control the damaging thought patters that engage your fear and prevent you from experiencing something new. Always choose to think big and not small. You must believe it's possible if you stand any chance of progress. There have been so many things across centuries that others argued could not be done; yet time and again they have been proved to be incorrect as each one material-ised in the minds of dreamers and ultimately became their reality.

Have faith and trust your higher self, contemplate on what your ideal life will look like, this will help your spirit become stronger. Change the way you think, when you're deciding what you can and can't do, refuse to give in to your emotional self-doubt or be influenced by others, it's not their dream, they weren't given it, you were. Make this your own personal stage, one where you decide to operate from the maximum state of existence.

YES, you can achieve all your visions. You can change your journey and your story. This is your ship to sail and with you at the helm, it becomes full of limitless possibilities. Change can be made in a second with a decision to start and a commitment to finish, engage in positive thinking habits, everything starts with a thought, it is your emotional connection to that thought and the contribution towards its realisation that will make it your own reality. Reach for the stars and live every day without limits.

Choose to Climb

Quote

"All things that live inside the mind that dreams, can be made possible by unwavering belief, a determined heart and the drive to make it so."

Geraldine Mair

Affirmation

Today I choose to see the endless opportunities around me. They are everywhere and I fearlessly act on each one. My intuition takes me in the direction of rewarding blessings and creates new ways for me to move forward embracing my personal best.

Strategy

An opportunity in your life is simply a possibility until you act to make it your reality. Developing hidden potential in each one becomes a gateway to something even better.

1. Start with a new outlook by choosing not to dwell on any limitations that you believe your own thoughts are responsible for.
2. Give all your attention to the things that you want to see show up in your reality and move away from all the excuses that you are giving yourself for reasons that it won't work.
3. Spend 10 minutes every night just before falling asleep thinking and feeling what your desired reality will look like when it shows up. Consistent attention to anything is what moves energies and this will keep the momentum flowing in the right direction.
4. Nothing is going to fall into your lap so don't wait around for that to happen, focus and a drive to succeed are the qualities required to change any outcome. Write one small action each day that will move you toward your dream... and just do it.

20. Know Your Value

If you are not aware of your own value and worth in this world, don't expect someone else to calculate it for you. Stop putting others first over your own wellbeing, why would you go to the extent of crossing miles for someone that wouldn't jump a fence for you. Always remember to process what you are being given in this world by others, versus what you truly deserve.

So often you are afraid to take time for yourself, you worry that you will be perceived as selfish or conceited, but the actual truth is, if you do not invest in yourself you will never really know your true worth. Once you understand that you matter, that you are important, and that you deserve it, everything changes.

The risk of burn out is real in this society, doing too much for others with no return can be exhausting. Be kind and offer help, but know your limits, it's too easy to get caught up in situations that neither serves or enriches you as a person. Refuse to be a doormat for anyone; these people are not respecting your value or your boundaries. Their time is not more important than yours, so be careful that you do not fall into the trap of being used or taken for granted, at the expense of your own health.

It starts with you, decide what you will accept make it non-negotiable and others will soon learn to respect your time. It makes no sense to always be second when you know you're good enough to be first.

Always make a commitment to treat others with respect, to be able to command the same. Civility costs you nothing and rudeness is distasteful to most. Your maturity will develop once you know when to say no or when to walk away by refusing to compromise your own value, means you will no longer find it necessary to give any discounts to those who wish to exploit it. Instead, you will place yourself behind the glass cabinets where they keep the valuables instead.

Quote

"Do not put the responsibility onto another to validate your worth; it's your job alone to inform those people of your true value."

Geraldine Mair

Affirmation

I am filled with light, love and peace. I treat myself with kindness and respect and expect the same from others. I know my own worth in this world. I stand by all the values that I have set out for myself. I choose to give my time to those who appreciate me. I am a good person and I stand by my convictions. I refuse to change to be accepted. I will stay true to myself and the right people will love me for it.

Strategy

No one can tell you what your value is, only you can show the world what you will accept or not.

1. Never compare yourself with anyone, and never worry about being accepted by others.
2. Schedule, *YOU TIME* into your life and make it non-negotiable.
3. Do not accept a message you know in your heart to be untrue.
4. Place a high level of importance on who you are.
5. Do not allow another person to bully, belittle or berate you.
6. Read, learn and practice how to be assertive.
7. Rejoice in your uniqueness and refuse to be pushed into a corner.
8. Pursue a worthy goal and strive to show your amazing self.
9. Write a description of the person you would like to be, and act like that person *NOW*.

21. Heart of a Warrior

It is in the darkest times in your life that you come to discover just how strong and resilient your heart is. It is built to withstand so much pain, so many tests, and things that you imagine you would never be able to survive yet against all the odds you do.

Your strength is beyond the confines of your own consciousness. The more threatened and challenged you feel the more opportunity you give for your warrior heart to emerge. There will be many times you will remember moments of incredible pain and you wondered how you ever got passed it...You always do.

You have an internal compass that drives you through enormous discord, yet it lies dormant inside each one of you until you need it to surface in your darkest moments. When bad things happen in your life and you become pushed to the very edge of the cliff looking down into the abyss, it is then that the person you were built to be, kicks in to action.

Your survival instinct will search everywhere for a solution and a reason to carry on and you will find it.

You fight to protect your honour; you will keep going in the face of every adversity because you fundamentally understand the precious gift of your life. You will find an inner resonance with strength that you tend to mostly ignore; yet it shows itself every time you are ready to give up or give in.

When you delve deep into your very soul, and search for the power that you need in that moment, you will always discovery it because that is what a warrior does. But remember it is not just accessible to you in times of hardship; it is available to you always, whenever you choose it. Harness your capacity for strength regardless of the situation at hand; it will see you through many trials and successes if you choose to utilise it.

Quote

"Every one of us has a warrior heart that wants to rise up and declare victory over any situation; this is the voice of the human spirit rising like a phoenix."

Geraldine Mair

Affirmation

I can find an answer to any problem. I have incredible resilience inside of me that knows no bounds. I know when I have a problem I simply need to quiet my mind and I will find the answer. I am a warrior.

Strategy

There will always be times when you feel that your limits have been reached. You will crumble and fall, however now you must realise that it is not in the falling that you become defeated, it is in the failure to rise that you are beaten.

1. Any stumbling block that pushes you back is only an opportunity to reflect on past trials that you have already overcome.
2. If you fall, get up! If you fall seven times then you must be prepared to get up eight. You were built to overcome your challenges and there is nothing that you cannot face.
3. Get support if you need to from another person who can give you a helping hand or a strong arm. It will only be in keeping all these things inside of yourself that you will become overwhelmed and find it very difficult to move forward.
4. No mountain is insurmountable unless you choose to make it so. Your life is waiting, so choose to climb.

22. The Pursuit of Happiness

If you believe every day that nothing wonderful is ever going to happen, you'll most probably be right. You draw to yourself that which you focus on with intent and belief. If you define your joy by a quest for anything external to yourself, there is very little chance that you will ever find the contentment or happiness that you seek. When you are in a constant state of striving feeling that you need additional things to make you whole, you are refusing to live in the moment, you are unaware of all the blessings around you, failing to participate in any gratitude for that which you already have.

Yes, you will feel a sense of gratification when you gain that which you are motivated to attain, however material aims only give this joy for a short period of time before you are aimlessly striving for your next fix. When you find joy in the simple things, the things that cost nothing; love, health, friendship, etc., you give yourself permission to embrace the euphoria of life. Admiration for lovely things is a normal response in anyone, though you should be careful, not to let too many things that resemble competition or rivalry enter your frame of reference and cause you to feel lack for something in your own life.

The balance of gratitude for what you have now, with the motivation to gain something better that will enrich you, will give you the peace that you seek in this life. Those who choose this path are more likely to live their lives with a higher level of fulfilment and the gift of happiness. You get to choose, it's your decision, because it is an inside job. Yes, there will be times in your life that you may feel sad, challenged or stressed but do not allow these to manifest as your normal states.

There isn't a person on this planet that would consciously choose to be unhappy, yet everyday so many people look for the very things that make it so. Everyday can be as beautiful as you choose to make it. It takes no more effort to look for the good than it does to perpetuate the bad, though it can have a massive impact on your life. Make the right choice for you and your family with each new day, and *choose to climb.*

Quote

"The pursuit of happiness can be found inside each of us when we stop and disconnect from all the distractions, appreciating fully what we have in our lives in that moment."

Geraldine Mair

Affirmation

I am content and happy. I choose to be the best example of myself every day that I present to the world. I see the miracles in my life and remember always that I am one. I am responsible and accountable for my own joy and bliss.

Strategy

So many of us look outside to blame situations and circumstances for our state of mind, when you become accountable to any event that is playing out in your reality you have the potential to act and alter its destination.

1. Keep guard at the door of your mind and do not allow anything to disrupt your peace, if this happens you lose your power and any control you have over the current moment.
2. Try to be around people who lift you higher instead of being with those who tear you down. Your whole life can change with this one small strategy. Those of us who are too easily influenced need to take this onboard even more.
3. Generate a sense of meaning in your life by choosing to take control of any discord. If you are in a situation that you feel is affecting you own demeanour, whether it be your career, a relationship or financial worries use this as a sign to take massive action to begin to correct it.
4. When you feel that you have taken responsibility for events that are repressing you it give happiness a chance to thrive once more.

23. Letting Go

Do you find yourself plagued by memories of your past? Then this passage is for you, though only if you're ready to let go, and only if you want to know that making peace with the past can help to set you free.

When you focus on regrets, sadness, grief or revenge for a very long time it grows in your reality. You will become depressed by the very weight of that which you choose to hold onto. The things that you recall are your own thoughts associating an event in the past that left an emotional scar.

When you give energy to that time it continues to show up in your experience. If you are angry or hurt now, you are choosing to remember the discomfort associated to that time or event in your life. Often you may not be aware you are doing this, but unconsciously this is what keeps the past and the pain alive in each present moment.

Give yourself permission to move forward, accept your memories, but do not clutch onto anything that you can no longer affect... What purpose does that really serve? Release the grip and drop the weight of the sack that you carry by letting it go. Be open to the possibility of allowing this energy to flow through you rather than staying stuck.

Expect to feel different, but do not define your life by any limitations. If you stay in the past you are only competent of living the rest of your life as a mere fraction of what you are truly capable of.

Life will continue to toss many trials and tribulations onto your path, and even after they are over they will remain in your memory, the most important thing is that you remember they do not define *you*. Be mindful of how your thoughts keep you stuck in an awareness that does not serve your higher self and you give opportunity for the pain of the past to heal. Let go and... *Choose to Climb.*

Quote

"If you do not let go of your past hurts, it will infect every other future moment you are blessed to experience in this life."

Geraldine Mair

Affirmation

I am love, I am lovable, I can release any anger in my heart and I move forward with strength and a commitment to give myself permission to let go and be happy again without reservation. I am blessed.

Strategy

With each new day you need to be willing to wipe the slate clean whenever you need to, daily if necessary. Start again without any condemnation or personal punishment of not being worthy enough to stay on your new path. As with any new habit it takes time to become your new reality. With repetitive action and a new perspective your future can be a whole lot brighter.

1. Take back your personal power by forgiving anyone who has hurt you, knowing that when you choose to do this, you are not condoning bad behaviour, you are allowing yourself the platform to let it go so it has no hold over you anymore. Say out loud with feeling: "[*Persons Name*] I forgive you".
2. Take back your personal power and forgive yourself. Step into a new reality knowing that your past mistakes, or those you have hurt, have no grip over you unless allow it. Say out loud with feeling: "[*Your Name*] I forgive you".
3. Everyday write one thing that you are letting go of and mean it, once it is released do not engage or talk about it anymore, allowing an internal shift to occur drives the focus onto better more positive things that require your attention in that moment and a feeling of purpose returns.

24. Gaining Perspective

People are consumed every day with their problems, they think about them; they talk about them, all the time, perhaps to whomever they meet... They focus all their energy on them, and are then often left wondering why they keep on showing up in their experience.

Think of this for a moment, if you were all to throw your respective problems into a big pile in the middle of the floor, so each of you could see what everyone else was going through, you would probably grab yours back. Everyone has baggage, but a healthy perspective can greatly alter the vantage point that you view it from.

People say that motivation and a positive attitude doesn't last, but in the words of Zig Ziglar, "that's why it's recommended that you do it every day like bathing". It requires a daily commitment and an adjustment in direction.

Change is hard for most; you would all rather stay within the confines of your comfort zone, which is the place you say you feel safe. However, if you search your soul you will soon discover that by not daring to step out of that box, you are fading, staying locked in a place of routine and stalemate... remaining here robs you of the ability to create the platform necessary for you to grow.

Expansion is the nature of our universe, there are beautiful memories just waiting to be made in your future, when you take a chance on something different from the norm. Remember your life is a magical adventure, a huge big canvas that you can use to create a beautiful picture or you can choose to leave it blank with very little on it, but why would you? Throw all the paint that you can at it and look back on a life that is overflowing with a kaleidoscope of colour, without regrets, without complaining and with immense gratitude and pride for the person you have chosen to become. Rise up and reach for your summit.

Quote

"Complaining every day is a waste of energy, inviting unhappiness and dissonance into your reality. Put as much effort into solving it as you do talking about it and your life will alter exponentially."

Geraldine Mair

Affirmation

I am positive. I am a force for good. I choose to see the beauty of each new day. I feel blessed to have more moments that I can experience and create wonderful memories. I am part of an ever-expanding universe and I participate fully in the miracle of my life.

Strategy

If you change your perspective on one small thing each day, at the end of a month you will have altered 30 things. With enough repetition it will become uncomfortable for you to be around anyone that is toxic, including yourself. When you make a conscious decision to set new standards for your life and make them non-negotiable, you set a different effect in motion.

It doesn't really matter where you start; just make a commitment to start now, where you are with what you have.

1. Decide now, right now to commit to stop complaining or moaning 'about anything' for the next 30 days.
   - No excuses, if you complain out loud to someone else, reset the 30-day timer.
   - No denial, if you find yourself moaning to yourself through your own self-talk about that which is wrong in your life, then immediately start to look for the good instead and say, "Thank You" for it.

25. Celebrate Your Uniqueness

When you judge yourself, you will often find that on reflection you are your biggest critic and this can in turn really pull you down. Think about what you say to yourself, about yourself, when you are by yourself; you are all doing it. Choosing to look at your reflection in the mirror, giving all your attention to the flaws, it's a common affliction that so many of you are engaging in. You can be the most beautiful person in the world to so many others but if you can't see it yourself, none of it will matter.

Every second that you spend criticising yourself and looking for every tiny fault that you dislike is a second of your life wasted, it is a moment of your life you can never get back. You don't have forever so stop wasting any of that precious time giving your energy and oxygen to these things.

Each of us are different and unique, though when you spend so much time in negative self-analysis you don't see the people who love and accept you for who you are. Be careful not to give too much of your focus to those who openly vocalise what they do not like about you. Not everyone is going to be your biggest fan and that's ok, instead give your effort to the people that make you feel good instead... there is no one out there that can make you feel unworthy unless you allow them to.

Everyone is beautiful, and you are born with a set of skills and talents that can and do change the lives of others every day. Your only job is to engage in the development of yourself to guarantee the best version of you, one you can be proud to show to everyone that you meet. If you can carve out a little time every day to work on that, the passing comments or gossip of others will have no influence over you.

Be an inspiration to people, use your time wisely, grow your confidence and know that you have much to contribute. Ignore the negative vibes and remember how wonderful you are, choose life, choose love, choose joy and choose gratitude. You are a miracle, like each one of the billions of people you share your beautiful planet with. Celebrate your uniqueness; someone loves you very much because of it.

Quote

"Do not waste another moment of your precious life trying to be the cheap copy of another. Step into your own greatness and let that light illuminate the world."

Geraldine Mair

Affirmation

I am a unique individual; I no longer need or have the desire to conform to another's expectation. I will be true to myself as much as I can. I will be the best example to others of how I deserve to be treated. I am grateful for the miracle that I am and I enter each new day knowing that I have a special purpose in this life and I intend to honour that.

Strategy

When you question your place here at any time throughout your journey, when you feel compromised or defeated by your own or another's actions. Remember there is no one else like you and you have much to bring to this world.

1. Spend time listening to positive podcasts, webinars or motivational speakers that are all readily available for free on the internet.
2. Commit to making a promise to yourself that you will refuse to listen to any negative comments about yourself from others.
3. If you think that there is a need for you to change, to present a better version of you to the world, then work towards that and start now.
4. Do not be discouraged by any naysayers or those who openly tell you that you have no capacity or drive to be different.
5. Make this the force that drives you. Show them through your own example that you have greatness within you, the right people will be waiting to help you on your journey and lift you higher.

26. Finding Empathy through Loss

Emotions are indicators of vibrational discord; they are useful to you and should never be squashed or ignored. Feeling the real physical pain of grief is not the same as becoming stuck in the emotion that prevents peace.

In fact, when you don't allow certain feelings to rise to the surface, you are repressing the pain internally and this can cause illness to flourish and prevent any shift from taking place. The first thing to remember about this emotion is that everyone should grieve on their own terms. No one has the right to judge or dictate when and how you should participate.

However, there should always be a space to talk things through with a trusted friend, a family member or a therapist. Sometimes it can be this very act that can help to bring perspective to a situation. It can also allow you to realise that you are not alone and the necessary support will be there if you wish to exercise it. Try to view it through a different lens, by doing so you become ready to seek a level of peace and acceptance for any experience that cannot be altered.

You're on a journey; you have a story that is different from anyone else. Those that you love come in and out of your life in divine order and that will be your personal experience of your time here. There is no approved list to merit how bad something affects you depending on the level of trauma. You will be completely overwhelmed by the death of a parent or a child, for others your grief may be rooted in losing a family pet, the loss of a job or business, or your family home.

Your feelings are your feelings and no one else can truly judge them, so choose to stand in your own power, listen to what your own mind and body is telling you it needs and respond accordingly. Stay in gratitude remembering how blessed you are for what has shown up in your experience, regardless of how long or short it was. Remember there is light after the darkest of storms, even with all the challenges that you must face life is still a wonderful gift. *Choose to climb*

Quote

"You need to find a greater meaning within the challenges that shift your perceptions of life. For it is only when you cannot reconcile that pain in yourself, or recognise it in others, that you lose your humanity."

Geraldine Mair

Affirmation

I am grateful for all the love and opportunities I have experienced in my life. I am strong enough to overcome any storm. I give freely of myself to others in pain, as I too understand their suffering. I give myself permission to spend as much time as I need to gain perspective and move forward.

Strategy

It can often be difficult to see the wood for the trees when you feel a personal loss, you must try however hard it is to find the joy again. You may never be the same person as the one that was evident before the loss, but you have an opportunity to grow from it and in spite of it.

1. In the giving of yourself to others, even when you are lost and in a dark place, it can help lift you out of the hole.
2. Try not to get caught up in the cycle of guilt as you become a prisoner to this emotion and find it difficult to move forward.
3. I have lost many personal things in my own life, through very difficult circumstances and it hurts to the very core. I focus on the gratitude for the experiences it brought me. I remember that I have been influenced in a positive way because it was all a part of my story.
4. *Choose to Climb* out of the pain into your joy once more, know that you will be alright and you deserve to give yourself the gift of happiness again.

27. How to Deal with Obstacles in Life

Obstacles in your life are designed to help you to develop your resilience and your perseverance. You cannot get mentally strong without them; to grow strength of character it's important to learn the lessons that life teaches you and how to respond to them. Everyone wants the spirit of a climber, but some fear the climb or the mountain may be too big to conquer, so why bother doing the work to get there. Anything worthwhile takes time, commitment and a desire for a worthwhile conclusion.

Your mountains are your obstacles, they can present themselves as events, circumstances or people; If you have been betrayed, hurt or offended, somewhere along the line you must release that anger and find it in your soul to absolve them; this is the true testament of character building. It does not make you weak, it does not give others permission to abuse you and it certainly doesn't mean that you are condoning bad behaviour. It is the necessary act that you should all take to regain control by refusing to allow it to control you.

You are bigger than your circumstances and obstacles simply remind you that you possess the ability to overcome. Exercising this ability supports your personal growth and truly demonstrates the courage of the human spirit that is in you. Find your way around, over, under or through, you have the capacity to triumph over anything, the bigger the problem the more satisfaction can be found when you conquer it. When you are interested you will do what is convenient, but if you are committed to finding a solution you will do whatever it takes!

You also possess the ability to inspire others by the way you handle a challenge, with honour, with dignity, and with grace. You cannot change another's behaviour, but you can create influence with ethical standards that others may choose to follow. Many things come into your life to teach you lessons about yourself, however rarely do you recognise obstacles, (events, circumstances or people) as teachers; when you learn to do so you will learn from every single one.

Quote

"Never waste a second of your precious time getting into an argument with an idiot, for in the end the only thing that you will achieve is that you too will become one."

Geraldine Mair

Affirmation

I am the example of the standards that I choose to accept for me. I am calm, I am peace, and I can deal with any difference of opinion in a dignified way. When others lose their calm, I choose not to for I know that when I lose my peace I lose my power.

Strategy

The only result that you have when you react to anything is a bad atmosphere, an uncomfortable silence or in the worst-case scenario the inability to fix the problem altogether.

1. You can only ever diffuse any heated situation, moment or experience with calm, this takes time and practice if you have always been used to reacting.
2. Take a moment when faced with any challenge in your life... Try to look at it from different perspectives, turn the problem over to your subconscious through thinking on it, and the solution will appear.
3. When the obstacle involves another person learn to communicate more effectively with a mature approach so you can find the solution that you seek. Ask questions and try to diffuse it with empathy and an understanding from the other's perspective.
4. View every challenge as a lesson in waiting; imagine yourself and how you will feel when you conquer it and you will develop the ability to find the answer.

28. Important Relationship Moments

How do you acknowledge your partner when you wake up in the morning? Do you tell them each day that you love them, not just a set of words that you say from repetition, but a feeling that comes from the heart? Do you still compliment them?

When they leave for their journey to work do you tell them to have a great day? Send them off with a loving embrace? It really doesn't matter what words you use, just send them a clear message that they are still loved by you, and you find them attractive. There are so many couples who lose that spark, the one that was so prevalent in the beginning, where you would have gone to the ends of the earth for each other.

If you are going through a difficult time in your own relationship, have you forgotten what it feels like to give and receive an intense hold, a passionate kiss, a genuine smile? These are all things that a person will hold onto all day long during the times that you are apart, and create excitement at the end of the day when they get to see you again.

Focusing your attention on words of encouragement to begin with, means, "to make courageous". When you speak positively to others you are instilling courage into the other person. Life has a way of draining 'it' out of you and it's easy to shut down, withdraw or get discouraged. When you tell your loved ones how much they mean and how proud you are of them, that extra energy and focus can release some untapped potential and you will both feel 'it'.

If they have a meeting, a presentation or an opportunity, let them know you believe in them and you anticipate a positive outcome. This will influence their own internal dialogue, for example if they're having doubts; encourage them to have faith in their goal. Knowing that no matter what happens each day in life, if you have someone who lifts you higher, supports you through everything, and makes you feel like the most important person in the world, it can transform the very nature of the relationship of those two people and provides a platform for a happier future that is very difficult to topple by anything external.

Quote

"When you choose to remember that very thing that attracted you to your partner in the beginning and you remember it with feeling; harness this emotion and it's possible for it to last a lifetime."

Geraldine Mair

Affirmation

I am love. I am a loving husband/wife/partner, I choose to make myself and the family my priority, I am grateful every day for the blessing that is my life and those whom I get to share it with.

Strategy

Happy contented couples never look outside of their relationship to validate their worth. Invest your efforts and time in the life partner that you have chosen and create a platform and the time necessary to guarantee your future together. Children, ageing parents, careers and obligations can all get in the way of carving out the time needed for a healthy team to flourish.

1. Make your relationship a priority, always.
2. There is nothing more rewarding than the love of another person that has grown over many years of understanding and mutual respect. Regardless of your commitments there is always the time if it's important enough to you!
3. Have a date night, free from work and children; everyone can do this once a week or even once a month.
4. Make the space in your life to connect with your partner; to get the relationship to a stage where both have room to grow and develop and your future together will be an amazing adventure, not just for the two of you but for your whole family.
5. Setting a loving example to your children gives them the impetus to emulate your lead so when they make their own connections with others, it ensures that they will be able to find the right fit.

29. Being Open to New Experiences

This year make a promise to try original and exciting things, there is an inexhaustible supply of adventures that you can have in your work and your personal life when you choose to seek them out, there is nothing of this world that can be more satisfying. Finding things that motivate and inspire can create momentum like a fully stoked furnace, don't do it with the intention to impress, do it for you. It's about impact, positive influence and inspiration.

Thoughts create action and this delivers results, the passion you have for your own interests can influence others and will be clearly visible, you can be an inspiration to many just by example and the way you choose to live your life. When you are open to new possibilities it can have a domino effect on those around you, and it is often these people that many others will avidly follow and choose to admire. Living with purpose and passion is often the very thing that will persuade others to try new things too.

As you navigate your path throughout life, be open to learning from those that you respect, try to do this with an element of childlike wonder. Life has the chance to be much brighter when you continuously acquire new skills, with the intention of expanding your knowledge to equip you with tools that can lead you towards a new direction.

If you are failing to consider ideas from others that are often better than your own, be aware that these thoughts are often routed in ego, which you excuse as pride or stubbornness because you believe that your way is either the right way or the best. This year try to get involved with people who challenge your own ideals and allow them to inspire you. Listen to other suggestions and realise that sometimes people come in and out of your lives to show you something new and exciting, so don't fight against the tide trying to change things that do not serve your higher good, just turn your boat around and get into the flow of life by choosing to sail downstream instead.

Quote

"Don't settle for experiencing your life as a passenger; learn to set expectations for your life as an explorer.

Derek Mair

Affirmation

I am open to new experiences in my life. I accept that others have valuable teachings that I can always learn from. I am intelligent and have an array of skills that are unique to me; I will share those skills freely to inspire others. I will always try to come from a platform of cooperation and not competition.

Strategy

Don't stop learning the moment your formal education ends. This is a fundamental flaw in our society. Seek new opportunities and new possibilities that push you beyond where you are; this ensures true personal growth in any chosen field.

1. Find a topic or subject that interests you, it's never too late to learn anything new. Personal development creates expansion of your own awareness and the potential to touch many other lives, so they too can gain a different perspective.
2. Decide to learn one small thing every day through self-help books and you will have amassed three hundred and sixty-five learning's in only one year. Just imagine how that could alter the trajectory of your own life.
3. Listen to audio books when you are in the car, choose a subject that genuinely interests you, like a new language or personal development or business skills. It has been statistically proven that listening to information over many hours whilst driving can be the equivalent of a college diploma.
4. Choose to accept new experiences or the ideas of another and you will be open to growth, change, and acceptance.

30. Dealing with Disappointment

When things go wrong in life, which they inevitably will, how will you cope? Should you be angry and bitter? Or could you still look forward to each new day and the possibilities ahead? While this is normal for me, I realise that not everybody feels that way.

Being an optimistic person is always looking for the best in any situation and expecting good things to happen. Optimism is the tendency to believe, expect or hope that things will turn out well. Even if something bad happens like the loss of your job for example, an optimist will always choose to see the opportunity hidden in the message. They see the potential to take their life down another path.

There have been many studies conducted within psychology that can show an encouraging impact on mental health if you look at your life and experiences from a different vantage point. It's no secret that when you are a more upbeat, forward-thinking individual it can impact your physical health too. When you are happy and have an expectation of better it strengthens the immune system, cardiovascular system and the body's ability to handle stress.

Pessimists think the opposite way however. They blame themselves or others for the bad things that happen in their lives and think that one mistake means more will inevitably come. They generally think that if something positive does happen it must have been a fluke that was outside of their control or a lucky streak that probably won't happen again.

You each have a choice in every moment, yes there will be disappointments that you will have to overcome, but facing things head on, putting strategies and solutions into place will guarantee a better conclusion and a shorter time that you may have to endure the moment. Staying stuck simply disempowers you from even finding the answer because at an unconscious level you are expecting someone else to rescue you. Remember you are all strong enough to face any adversity. Search inside and know that it is already there.

Quote

"Nothing keeps you stuck in this life more than an attitude that is unwilling or open to change."

Geraldine Mair

Affirmation

I am an optimist. I choose to know I have the capacity to see the lesson in everything when I open my eyes. Nothing can hold me back unless I give it the power to do so. Disappointments in refection are often gifts that take me to a place I may not have found otherwise.

Strategy

When you have a choice in anything, why not try to make it one that empowers you towards the best outcome. If you continue to do what you always have you will never find a better solution as the outcome will always be the same.

1. The only way your life can be miserable on a constant basis is because you decided to give all your energy to the pursuit of that goal.
2. Stop! Think for one moment and ask yourself, "how is this affecting my life?" then take the necessary steps to alter your destiny path by choosing to see things with a different lens.
3. The only person who has the capacity to change is you, no one else can do it for you, make a conscious decision that allows you to recognise that you are unhappy where you are and real transformation has the chance to happen.
4. Climb every single time you are disappointed, learn the lesson and accept fully that your best days are still out in front of you.
5. Think the best, be your best, strive for the best. Expect the best in every situation and... *Choose to Climb!*

31. Design Your Life

Designing your future is the most important project that you will ever be responsible for, if you are not willing to control that part of your life, you run the very real risk of slotting into someone else's plan for you instead. When you take ownership for your choices towards that creation, it guarantees you the opportunity to get the most from the talents you've been given. If you restrict it though, it can have a heavy impact further down the line on the evolution of your own life.

Like sliding doors there are always two destinations at the fork in the road. Happiness or unhappiness is often a matter of selection. You should endeavour to create the kind of life that not only looks good to others but that fulfils you on the inside too. Free will is the very thing in each one of you that gives the potential for adjustment in any given moment. I believe that your attitude to anything that requires commitment, will ultimately determine your altitude and how far you can climb to attain them. If you have a burning desire for a future that looks different from the one you are currently experiencing, the first thing you need to deal with is your attitude. If you don't get that right, then your life is never going to reflect the image that you really want.

In many cases, people hold on so tightly to their past or to a repetitive pattern routed in fear it keeps them in perpetual limbo, please understand that you are creating this cycle and only you can modify it. There can be no movement until you reach a point in your life that has become so painful, the only option left is for a fundamental shift to take place. You can start now to turn the page and begin a new chapter, you have the authority to initiate this and no longer be at the mercy of anyone who is trying to hold the reins for you. Fertile soil lies on the other side and it is waiting for you to sow the seed of your new story. No matter what you cultivate, weeds or a harvest that is what will grow. Plant only good vital knowledge that is imperative for growth. You have the freedom to decide today and this can equip you with the tools to design your own destiny. What an amazing concept!

Quote

"The only restrictions placed on a life that is unfulfilled were created by you, when you change the viewpoint your life will alter in ways you cannot imagine."

Geraldine Mair

Affirmation

I am miraculous and I am a miracle. I choose a life of abundance and happiness. I am capable of change; I am the artist, composer and designer of my life. I am an example of how others should treat me. I am enough

Strategy

You have the potential to choose your life by design and not by routine and habit, by acknowledging this you will no longer settle for a life that does not inspire.

1. Unhappy at your job – start making plans today, update and send out your CV to potential employers that can use your skills, or if you are inspired enough start your own business and find out how from all the resources available on the internet in your area.
2. If you are afraid of change remember this is a healthy response, so if you want more that what you currently have, you will need to be ready to alter your attitude now.
3. Change is growth, get excited, get inspired and get educated in the necessary areas that will allow it to happen for you.
4. Make the jump; refuse to stay in any place that you feel you are dragging yourself out of bed for, on the other side of your habitual patterns is real freedom for the individual willing to take a chance.

32. Harness Your Potential

Everyone is given the amazing gift of infinite possibility when born into this world. As you grow all of you are driven by wishes and goals, a built-in navigation system with nothing but the desire to expand, this can be the catalyst for an amazing life or it can repress you if it is driven by fears.

There are many inspirational people who see the world as a beautiful place full of opportunity and potential. But there are too many who view it with a whole different perspective. They see obstacles, complications, hurt and pain, this view damages a happy soul and turns it into one of disappointment, one that is constantly waiting for all their internal beliefs to be realised by what their five senses are transmitting.

You each have the possibility to become happy and positive people, but allowing thoughts to mar your judgment, often leaves you open to a belief that the world is a bad place full of evil or corruption. When you buy into propaganda from news feeds or the social media circus, this only clouds your opinions further. If you nurture this belief you will not have a very high expectation for yourself or others and therefore you will be condemning yourself to a life devoid of joy.

Never allow too many views from external sources to penetrate far enough into your own mind, that you allow it to become your truth. The only way to harness the potential in yourself is to know your own mind first, protect your values refusing to compromise them to the degree that they are no longer visible. Choose the gift you received at the start of your life, a perfect creation with boundless possibilities, know that you too can change direction at any time, with enough conviction you can see things very differently indeed. Step into this reality and harness all your potential to make it so.

Quote

"There is no greater gift than the gift of life, what you choose to do with that gift is entirely your own good or bad."

Geraldine Mair

Affirmation

I can choose my own path. I am responsible for my own choices and the results they produce. I am blessed to have so many opportunities to express myself. I choose to follow my own heart and not the expectations of others. I have incredible potential, it has been my inheritance all along and I now engage fully with this gift and harness it all for my best life yet.

Strategy

It is so easy to become a follower instead of a leader, you have an instinctive desire to fit in but this is not a dream of our own life that you hold in our heart.

1. Live your life on your own terms, work towards goals that you have designed that do not violate your own values.
2. Life has its own ebbs and flows, you should be aiming for this, never try to gain acceptance through compromises, it's simply madness.
3. Find your own destiny by learning about yourself and what you really want versus what you are settling for and start to take the steps towards making it your reality.
4. Plan your life by setting standards that are non-negotiable especially for yourself and stick to them.

33. The Negative and Positive Side of Anger

First let us address the negative side of this powerful emotion, there are times in everyone's life where anger will fill them up and spill over in an overwhelming uncontrollable way but If you allow it to flow and pass over you it should not have a lasting effect. However, if you allow anger to consume, it will turn you inside out, it will court you, follow you, become a part of you and when you reach this point you will be responsible for inviting it in. A mindset that has stagnated like dirty water becomes infectious, poisonous, and full of deadly thoughts, this is hate and what anger becomes if you feed it.

Bring into reality your human side; let it go, so you can open the door to transformation and possibility. When you release and forgive yourself or others you will no longer allow this emotion to contaminate your thoughts and your life, by refusing to engage with this toxic state you prevent it from consuming your time and damaging your relationships.

There is also a very positive side to anger as well; it can be an emotion that fires up a diminished spirit, one that you are no longer prepared to tolerate anymore. It can often come about if you have felt restrained, sometimes for years, but when you reach your own personal limit, one that you cannot go below, it can bring about a deeply needed change that can manifest into a positive outcome.

When channelled in a healthy way it can be the vehicle that causes essential alterations to your life. This could be a difficult situation that you are struggling to move forward from. Sometimes it takes you to get angry enough inside, that you won't give up or give in and it will be a catalyst to push you through the perturbation to the other side. Be aware that this emotional feeling is an internal driving force and never directed at another. It is a fire that lights on the inside that now drives a fully charged engine with a desire for change to see it through to its end... *Choose to climb.*

Quote

"The only emotion that can neutralise anger in an individual is love and acceptance of a situation, diffusing the need to express the emotion in the first place."

Geraldine Mair

Affirmation

I choose to be a peaceful person. I remove myself from any conflict and will choose not to judge and remain neutral. I refuse to engage with toxic relationships that do not enhance my life experience. I will choose to make my interaction a positive one whenever I can.

Strategy

You will experience people that seem to always be angry with life or in the midst of a drama. If you don't know one it might be you. It is not your job to change who they are or the way they perceive the world. It's in your best interests to make a conscious effort to respond with a wiser head, as a real compromise can almost always be found from this approach.

1. When you react with anger you create more anger and conflict. Choose to respond with understanding, responsibility and a calm demeanour; it vastly improves your chances to defuse a situation with a mature result.
2. Stop trying to defend if you feel threatened, as this is a lose; lose situation, if you find yourself in this area, disengage and walk away until you are calm enough to deal with the issue properly.
3. If you feel that you are easily irritated and it creates explosive reactions in you, try to identify what triggers these emotions. Changing your circle, finding enjoyable hobbies and spending time in reflection can all help to gain perspective, so you can stop hurting yourself and others by your negative approach.

34. Nurture Whomever You Can

Our behaviour as humans often brings into question your actions for the better good of yourself and others. Most of the daily difficulties that you encounter are usually caused by your failure to ensure that people are encouraged within environments that nurture their wellbeing.

A heart that has toughened through years of disappointment becomes guarded, worried and fearful. Try to see beyond the mask, everyone has a story, a journey, and a life experience different from you. Are you ready to be their judge and jury? Are you qualified for that job?

Let each one of you be the catalyst for change within the communities that you inhabit. Immerse each person that you meet or know with inspiration, friendship and acceptance. Let's not jump to condone another because you measure them by your own standards, your personal experience of this world may be vastly altered from theirs, especially if you have had a privileged one; you don't choose your families they are given to you. They will be the first teachers and the building blocks that create the foundation of what or who you will become.

When you choose a platform of hope and encouragement everyone wins, including you. Go beyond what you have been taught, go further than your own conditioning and paradigms that keep you stuck in belief systems that still paralyse you and show those people what it feels like to be accepted and included. You are all accountable and you can all make a huge difference even if it is in the life of only one.

Your genes may be inherited from your parents but the same is evident of the environment you live in unless you choose to change. Love is all you have to keep you growing and moving towards a better tomorrow, rise higher in every action you undertake with the intention of making a noticeable difference. Follow your own path and act in that moment you feel inspired to do so regardless of what others think of you, letting go of external opinions will encourage a beautiful mind to flourish, for you will never rise any higher than the thoughts you propagate.

Quote

"In the end you are all human, you all feel, you all need, you all have the capacity to hurt and harm, remember that."

Geraldine Mair

Affirmation

I am love, I have the capacity to give encouragement, I can inspire others and myself in the process. Everyone is unique and I embrace those differences, I choose not to judge anyone by what I see with my eyes, but listen to my heart instead knowing I have the potential to make a positive impact in doing so.

Strategy

You are all conditioned through society, your parents, your peers, your friends and work colleagues. You all have a desire to be accepted and to fit in and you all have the capacity to alienate people when they don't fit with your ideals.

1. Do not judge another when you do not know their struggles and their challenges.
2. Show understanding, friendship and hope even if you must step away from the status quo.
3. Kindness is a gift that you are all graced with and you each have the capacity to elicit this in any situation that you know demands it.
4. Strength comes in choosing the right path. When your intuition alerts you to a behaviour you are engaging in to hurt another, listen to it, your internal compass is never wrong and in that moment, you are wounding.
5. *Choose to Climb* showing there is always a better way even if it's not the most popular one.

35. Reflections on Loss

If you have had a difficult year or maybe you lost someone very close to you and you feel tested to your limits, don't lose faith, though no one can go back and make a brand-new start, anyone can start from now and make a brand-new ending.

Don't allow your past to drag you down. There is never any benefit to be had locking in painful memories that prevent you from making any progress. Make a new choice with the conviction that you deserve to be happy, embrace your strengths and individuality, be the best that you can be and know that if your desire is strong enough you will find the power through support, love and faith to move forward.

When you remember your past, it creates memories to reflect upon, some will be wonderful and take you back to a time of pure joy, others will have been painful times but still you got through it. Take the good with you and learn from the painful lessons but don't be tempted to unpack your suitcases and live there.

Pain can test you in very different ways, it can bring you to your knees or it can make you stronger. Life by its very nature must come to an end in this place, but there is always a presence of that which was lost, this can never die, as it is a part of who you become for having known those whom you loved.

Living gives you the opportunity to contribute to that life, keeping memories alive and celebrating how it has moulded you. When someone is lost it takes time to accept the change and it is a painful lesson to overcome, but you must if you are to enjoy living once more.

Seize every opportunity to have an amazing life, you are only here for a short time so live in the moment and be thankful for all of it. To all those who have gone before you this is what they would truly want for your life.

Quote

"To love another person and to share in those life experiences, enhances every aspect of our existence, it's a beautiful blessing for having had the opportunity to share in that passage no matter how long or short it was. No longer being able to see them doesn't mean that you forget, they're just not supposed to be physically in your story for the remainder of your journey."

Geraldine Mair

Affirmation

I give myself permission to move forward through my life's story embracing all the wonderful things I have still to experience. I remember with love always the special people that have impacted my life in a positive way and because of this I now live in expectation of the best.

Strategy

It can be a wonderful gift to reflect on your life and those you have had the privilege of sharing it with in all its forms, from family to colleagues, from associates to strangers who created an impression by crossing your path.

1. Find the happy memories that illicit strong emotion to help to bring about peace once again.
2. Human beings tend to focus in the earliest days of loss on the tragedy that brought it about, this is a perfectly natural response and in time you can change the trajectory of this vision, setting you free from the pain. In the months ahead if you can remember these words you will come to smile on all the amazing moments that have enriched your life through the connection of another.
3. You never stop missing those special souls you just learn a different way to cope. Get around people who have also lost that you can express your deepest fears to, it will help you to gain strength knowing that you are never alone and that once the clouds clear, in time you will see the sun again.

36. Taking Responsibility and Be Accountable

When you don't take one hundred percent responsibility for your own life you block your own progress and happiness. Using your creative power to be a proactive participant in your life allows you to transcend limitations and live in joy.

It's impossible to love anyone more than you love yourself. It's easy to love yourself when you feel good, look great and everyone cooperates. The real test comes with accepting your flaws, and loving your humanness. Self-love allows you to heal those parts and move forward into a brighter light and deeper appreciation for yourself and others.

Become your own priority. Not from a selfish perspective but in the realisation that if you do not invest into yourself, whether through education, physical health, and mental wellness you're at risk of burnout.

It's so easy to just get overwhelmed with life especially when you put too many pressures on yourself, this can make life difficult to cope with until it is too late. It can feel as if everything is caving in on you.

Look after your body, mind and spirit, taking responsibility with scheduled breaks throughout your day. Feed your mind with inspirational knowledge, books and videos. Help those around you, as there is no better way of lifting the spirit in knowing that you have contributed positively to another person, massively improving your own positive vibration.

Make sure you are prioritising the company of those who raise you higher and inspire you, when you spend time with anyone who accepts you there will never be any need for you to defend your actions, and therefore no threat to your joy. Celebrate all your wins and be grateful for what you have, no matter how small you think it is. Even in our greatest challenge there are others who are suffering more. You must take responsibility for all the actions and decisions you are making because the alternative is that you will learn nothing, unless you are prepared to take full ownership of the life you are creating. Always choose to climb higher on this journey you call life and be accountable for you.

Quote

"Denying any action, you have personally committed with the intention of offending another is grave indeed."

Geraldine Mair

Affirmation

I am responsible for all my actions and decisions. I am accountable for my own life. Being helpful is one of the most rewarding actions there is. I invest in me so that I can bring my very best each day by taking full responsibility for my life.

Strategy

No one has any respect for those who continue to dodge bullets and put others under the bus. Be the one that others choose to emulate, be the example for how it is done with grace and style.

1. Give people the chance to follow your lead to aspire and to learn from you, be the person whom others speak highly of about your integrity.
2. Continue to grow yourself through sustained learning, focus on positive and inspirational material, as this will enhance your life immensely.
3. Stay away from toxic and negative environments unless you find yourself in one, use it as a platform to encourage change, this is no easy feat but change can only begin when one person stands up and is prepared to be heard regardless of the response.

37. Living With Passion

Life is your journey, you will fall, but you have the capability to rise, you will make many mistakes, but you will hopefully learn from them. You are an imperfect human, and you will have been hurt by others and you will have hurt them. You are alive and what a precious privilege this is for all of us every day. Get up every morning and chase the things you love.

Don't leave anything on the table; beauty, excitement, experiences, events and journeys are all waiting for you. Keep striving for all the good that is already yours otherwise you risk missing what is just around the bend. Why should you put yourself through this? Because you're only here once and tomorrow is never guaranteed.

The good times are worth it, because they help you to be grateful for the experience. The bad times are worth it too, as they give you comparison and really make you appreciate all the good in your life, helping you to cope with challenges. God willing, you will get to experience many of them over the course of your life.

You are a very valuable asset and your contribution here makes all the difference to someone else's life, even if you are unaware of it. When you are still for just a moment and reflect on this you realise just how important you truly are. You are someone's miracle.

Living with passion encourages you to live your life fully with all the opportunities that present themselves to you, if you make only one decision this year then live without any fear in your heart, you control this movement, don't just dip you toe into the water, jump in and immerse yourself with all the exhilaration that brings. The bigger the splash, the better the result! Live with Passion!

Quote

"Be passionate about your life, understand the priceless gift your hold in your hand every moment and go out and share that with the world."

Geraldine Mair

Affirmation

I love my life. I love my family. I am grateful for my gifts. I am here to make a difference. I embrace each day with gratitude for the opportunities that it will bring; I am living every moment with passion.

Strategy

When you choose a life of mediocrity and you convince yourself that this is your lot in life, you are selling yourself very short of the potential that lies inside.

1. Each day no matter what it holds for you, be expectant, live in the moment and appreciate all that is around you and that you are a part of.
2. Settling should not become part of your vocabulary; you can live your live with passion each moment. Passion for your partner, Passion for your children, Passion for your gifts, Passion for your friends and your career.
3. Everything is a choice, when you become grateful you alter your perception, then you have the capability to change your world, it all starts in the mind.
4. What are you saying to yourself, about yourself when you are by yourself is your truth, change this and you change everything.
5. Express yourself through doing something that you love to do, make it a hobby or make it a career.

38. Becoming a Powerful Force

I believe that your imagination will always be stronger than anything you have learned or knowledge that has been given to you. I believe that the most influential avatars of the past knew how to harness this with their thoughts, long enough to engage an internal drive that created it into their reality. I believe that to dream of a better life or a peaceful world will always be more powerful than the facts you see every day on the news.

You hold the incredible ability to triumph, when you have an unwavering, unconditional love for anything. Hope can be a powerful force, and maybe there will never be any real magic in it but what I do know is that it holds a light inside you so bright, that no one can dim it. It gives you the drive to move forward regardless of the tests that you face, and it gives you a focus to stretch yourself enough that you start to believe in a better outcome beyond where you are now.

So, although there is no evidence for it, I like to think that it is a kind of magic that you have the capacity to tap into. When you harness that control allowing it to rise to the surface there is no other choice but to come out fighting and in doing so you can advance forward.

When you feel as if all seems lost having a hopeful mindset will never ever leave you defeated by any obstacle that life brings your way. When you feel as if you are in an endless pit it can be the only thing you have available to you and the one thing that can change the situation into a far brighter one.

Developing an expectation for a particular thing in life, guarantees you are always leading from the front using this principle. There is always an unending supply of second chances just waiting for you when you are ready to believe in a different approach. When you cultivate that powerful internal force you are no longer enslaved but empowered creating the momentum that raises the bar pushing you forward, so *Choose to Climb*

Quote

"There lies within each of you an invisible force, one that you can use that is so powerful it has the capacity to change your course."

Geraldine Mair

Affirmation

I believe I am a powerful individual with a capacity for growth. I have inside of me all the knowledge necessary to begin making better choices right now. I will never give up on hope, as I know it is the one thing that will keep me moving forward to the guiding light in the distance.

Strategy

When you lose hope you lose everything, there is no powerful energy available to you then, even the very desire to want something different is gone. You are in a state of limbo a kind of inertia; this is crippling and cannot help in any situation.

1. Write down on paper your future hopes and read them often.
2. To be an influencer for change become the person that can illicit the qualities others want to follow.
3. Look after your health and your mind if you wish to connect to all the potential that resides inside you.
4. Follow mentors that inspire and introduce you to concepts that you may never have been aware of, and teach others.
5. I have found amazing mentors by following the works of Louise Hay, Les Brown, John Assaraf, Dr Wayne Dyer and Anthony Robbins. I encourage you to look them up, their stories are inspiring and show how they harnessed their own internal force by altering their thought of mind that returned exceptional results.

39. Test of a Strong Resolve

It's true that even the toughest of times don't last forever, and if you remain strong you'll make it through and be able to weather whatever storms come your way.

The human spirit has shown that it's capable of making it through tough times, you are so diverse, you can search with everything you have to source a solution to any problem and there are endless stories from many people proving this. Even some you will already know.

The best part of dealing with hardship is that it toughens you up for the next trial in your life. You grow emotionally and spiritually when you are tested. You can't avoid these hurdles in life, nobody can as they are often due to circumstances beyond your control, but you do have a choice on how you handle it in the way you respond.

Knowing that you're only getting better with each new struggle can be an inspiration during those times when you feel like giving up. It's tricky when others around just seem to be sailing on through life, when you feel as if everything is falling in around you, but everyone has a different journey an alternative life story to your own and you have no idea what others are going through right now.

You can only work on yourself to embrace change; this is the best way forward to recover a tough resolve. You will all have your times of struggle, you are never given more than you can handle and with the right tools you can always endure it, no matter how rough the seas are.

Being a tough person doesn't mean you must be callous, insensitive or aggressive, it just means you have an inner strength that has been battle-tested. Never give up on anything that deserves your fight, these are the dreams that will create your future and can change your destiny.

Quote

"There will be many storms to navigate throughout life; set your sail high, catch each new wave, hold your course steady and your ship will always reach shore."

Derek Mair

Affirmation

Each day I am taking the steps to develop a strong resolve. I decide to be tender, compassionate, sympathetic and tolerant first with myself and then with others. I decide to never give up, and never give in, no matter how tough it gets. I decide that I have the strength and the conviction to succeed and live my life my way.

Strategy

Life will always throw a few curveballs in your direction, perhaps just when everything is starting to go well; something shifts and you end up with a spanner in the works...

1. Define the situation or problem clearly in writing.
2. Define the very worst possibly outcome to the situation.
3. Resolve to accept that the worst outcome could happen.
4. Begin to act to minimise the worst situation.

    • Use whatever you have at your disposal to find a solution that takes the sting out of the situation.
    • If you need help ask someone who knows more than you do about your problem and see if a solution can be found together.
    • Speak to a trusted friend or family member, often when you share your problems you get to see them from a different perspective, it allows a clearer vision so you can create a plan of action, halting the chaos in its tracks and giving you back control.
    • There is always a way through, a way round, a way over or a way under any problem; all you must do is ask.

40. Choosing a Better Attitude

There is no such thing as perfection in this life, and if you are expecting this environment you are setting yourself up for massive disappointment. You will have said things that you regret, so choose to learn from them and be gentle with yourself and others. When you spend time thinking about all the resentment and bitterness of past events or moments that you can no longer effect, you will poison your mind, your body and your spirit.

Forgiveness is the way to freedom, it puts the ball firmly back into your own court and it releases you from the constant baggage that gets carried around because of it. Your attitude can massively alter your course, take you out of the dark and into the light; this is a choice that is available to you always.

If you are truly committed to changing your mindset in the direction of a better life, it can be a great exercise to record all your amazing moments or great experiences in a journal. This gives concrete evidence even to the biggest sceptic amongst us that altering the way you think and act has a profound effect on your persona. Don't take short cuts and think you will be able to remember all the good that has come into your lives only in your heads; you will be unable to factually recall the many wonderful things that made you the person you are today. When your focus is towards improvement it amplifies your capability to see things from a better vantage point, creating the platform to receive more.

Re-reading a journal that you have created when you are feeling a little low can be used as a great pick-me-up in difficult times and an engine that keeps you searching for more during the great times. You will find that you will re-live the moments that you wrote about and this will raise your mood into a more positive one as it focuses on all the better-quality moments that happened but you may have forgotten about. Be a part of seeing the best in everything and everyone. Practise feeling gratitude every day and you will learn to have appreciation for your life every time that you think about what you have. The alteration of your attitude now is assured.

Quote

"When you are truly grateful for your lives and the opportunity to experience each new day, it opens up the floodgates for more."

Geraldine Mair

Affirmation

Today I decide to embrace a new attitude towards my life, my family and myself. I realise that change happens from within and it is in my power to action this at any moment. I am given a new chance every day to be thankful; the very gift of another day can be my first start of a real shift.

Strategy

When you focus all your energy on negative responses that is exactly what will become your reality.

1. Buy a journal like it suggests in the passage opposite, it needn't be anything fancy, and record just one thing each day:
    *   Something that you are grateful for
    *   An exciting experience or something good that happened

    Once you begin this process it won't be long before you will be able to think of many things that you can list.

The awareness of the little things brings you into the present; here are some examples to get you started. "I am grateful for the beautiful supportive family of which I am a part." "I am grateful for my hearing to listen to my favourite music." "I am grateful for my sight that allows me to see the beauty in my child's face."

You get the idea, so enjoy this process for it is one of the simplest of tasks that you can do to change your attitude from the moment you rise.

41. Pain Associated with the Grief on the Loss of your Partner

Grief can destroy you or it can focus you. You can decide that your life from this moment on is pointless since you were left alone because it ended in death, or you can rise knowing that sharing a deep connection with another human being was a wonderful gift that you had the chance to share.

When you reflect you will begin to see it was so much more than just the daily routines that you did together, it's all the little things that you put in as a team that made up years' worth of memories that you hold forever. When you lose someone very close to you that has shared your life intimately, you realise that it was everything.

You will come to understand that it was you're "WHY" that makes you feel the pain that you do. Why you chose them, why you built a life around them and with them, why you choose to have a family with them, take holidays with them and build dreams of a beautiful future with them. You realise that it was and is every event and precious moment of it.

What you will appreciate was the love that was shared in every decision that you made; the things that moulded you into a couple and created the foundations that you built a life upon.

When enough time has passed you will realise that the weight of what is gone can catch you unaware and drive you to your knees, not because of your grief and the weight caused by it, but for the amazing gift that this person became in your life and all the magical moments they participated in before they left.

You will always feel the ache, there is a place that no other can ever fill nor should they, but this can be replaced in time with an inner peace if you let it. You become immensely thankful for all those who have shared your life's journey and touched you in ways they can never know. Having the support of your family can be the first step you need to take to help you to heal. I understand this on a very personal level, and sharing your experience can truly help the process.

Quote

"There is no greater loss than those you have loved with your whole heart, but when a grateful mind remembers, peace can flourish once more."

Geraldine Mair

Affirmation

I realise what a blessing it has been to have been loved so freely by another person who chose me and accepted me for who I am. I know in time I can be capable of joy once more. I give myself permission to be at peace. I choose to remember all the good times and positive memories.

Strategy

When you think about those that are no longer physically here, it can bring emotions to the surface that can be difficult to overcome.

1. The best way through grief is with action, when you are ready to participate whether that be returning to work, taking up a new project or getting involved with a voluntary association it can help you to find your purpose once more.
2. Everything in life that has a massive impact on you will require self-care so take the time to heal.
3. Each one of us will handle it in a different way and there is no manual for this process. This is most certainly the one thing in life that you must do on your own terms, no apologies.
4. Those who care enough about your heart will understand you and never judge you.
5. Speak about your loved ones often as this keeps their memory alive in your life and the lives of others close to you, an important part of acceptance.
6. Find a safe space either with a group going through the same pain or a therapist that can offer personal time and a safe place to express yourself. This can help you to find joy and allow you to let go of any guilt.

42. We All Make Mistakes

There are times when you may have made a decision that was against your better judgment. If you have made mistakes, there is always another chance for you. You can choose a new beginning at any moment, isn't that a wonderful concept? Each day an opportunity to wipe the slate clean and begin again is there for you. Decide to make that commitment to yourself and refuse to continue looking behind at what has already gone, knowing the answer can never be found there.

There is no such thing as remaining stuck anywhere unless that has been your decision to do so, fear of change will keep you in a place that can become very uncomfortable if you stay there, yet so many of you take this path even though you claim it's the opposite of what you really want.

If the fear of failure is stopping you from moving forward, think about this for a moment. It is not in the falling but in the staying down. There is no such thing as failure in this life except the failure to participate. Once you get into action and refuse to be a victim success is inevitable. The best people have made many mistakes in life, but admitting it and refusing to repeat it guaranteed their progression. Your personal reflections on any weaknesses are only markers for lessons to be learned.

Never be overcome by woes, know that your highest rewards are on the other side of any test and it will be at this moment that the tide will turn. When you try an alternative tactic to anything that you have done in the past it gives a chance of a different result. When even the smallest of improvements are made you can move forward in confidence that you are heading in the right direction. Be grateful for trials that make you focus every day on something more positive. What a difference it can really make to your life when you learn to view experiences from this vantage point.

Quote

"Life is full of errors, mine and yours, but the lessons we can learn through them are vast."

Geraldine Mair

Affirmation

I will choose to forgive myself of my shortcomings that I may have made in the past, I realise that there can be no movement to anything better when I stay there. I move forward with confidence knowing that the power of change is at my disposal when I am ready to take it.

Strategy

When faced with any mistakes you make in life you will always have two choices. Step up or move over and allow someone else to make the difference.

1. Become the person that takes the reins; you have the skills, the capability and the strength to push through.
2. When you face your fears, they disappear like mist over a horizon.
3. When a mistake you made is holding you back, reprogram your subconscious by writing "I forgive you" read it often and let go of the energy attached to it in doing so you release yourself from its hold.... Like any muscle when exercised often enough a new you can emerge with a better outlook and a positive attitude.
4. *Choose to Climb* through your toughest moments, just remember back to a time that you didn't want to do something but you found the courage and the motivation, the feeling that followed was because you achieved you aim and it was magical.
5. This can become your reality each time you do something that frightens you. Make the leap, take the jump; the person that will emerge from this will surprise you. Keep growing, keep learning, and use any tools at your disposal to overcome any hurdle that life throws your way.

43. Building a Happy Life

Building a happy content life requires only a few simple things. You hold the potential in your hands to affect another with little gestures that create domino effects that can spread like wildfire. You always gravitate to those who elicit warmth and acceptance, the joy of being around that level of positive vibration affects your own. When you fail to live in the present you get too wrapped up in yourself, your past or your troubles and miss so many chances to impact the lives of others in doing so.

Happiness is not something outside of you; it is indeed an inside job. If you are looking for connection from others, first, you must give of yourself before expecting something in return. So many of us get this the wrong way around and wonder why disappointment always follows. Relationships are about what you can bring into it, not take away from it. Showing love to your children, your partner and your friends is a powerful expression of connection that creates happy well-rounded human beings, this kind of exchange always returns to the measure that it was delivered. Laughter is another important ingredient and the medicine for many ills in this world, life is just better when you're laughing and so much more fun when you express this emotion freely, there is very little else that I am aware of that has the curative qualities of this euphoric state.

If you have offended anyone and you are aware of it make it your goal to apologise, take responsibility and ownership for your misdemeanours. Failing to do so creates an uncomfortable atmosphere and if it festers for a long time can rapidly descend into real distain, ultimately affecting your health. Be mindful of this if you wish to open channels that start the healing process and protects relationships, the very foundation that all happiness is grown from. Spend no time in worry, hate, jealousy, fear, or despair, for happiness can never be found in these emotions. Care for others; accept those you see as different either through creed, race, or colour. You each have within you the capacity to influence another generation by adopting this in a very positive way. Children do what you do, not what you tell them to do so lead wisely with a happy heart.

Quote

"You can be cheerful or you can be sick and tired, a choice you make every day, it takes no more energy to be either but how you feel and how you impact others will be vastly altered by the decision you take."

Geraldine Mair

Affirmation

I choose happiness; I am a power for good. I am a positive influence on others. People enjoy my company and I have many wonderful things in my life that make me feel very blessed and grateful.

Strategy

Hopefully when you reflect on this passage you will see how important it can be to embrace happiness instead of its opposite.

1. Each day make it your mantra to be thankful for what the day will bring you. Develop an attitude of expectation and anticipation.
2. If there is anything in your life that is pulling you down either change it or move away from it.
3. Start today designing your new life, engage only with those who encourage you and lift you higher.
4. Spending time with people who berate you or belittle you can bring you no lasting joy; they will only leave you questioning your own personal worth, so choose your tribe wisely.
5. You always have a choice and it's always yours. Grow your courage and do not accept anything less than you know you deserve.
6. To be happy there are things in your own life that you may have to give up or release, people, possessions or goals that are restricting, hampering or stressing you, some things must be non-negotiable in order for you to thrive.

44. The Family

You can leave your family when you are grown, go out into the world to make your life, you can put miles of roads or countries or bodies of water between you, but you always carry them within you for they have contributed to who you are. When you are part of a loving family it's important to remember that forgiveness will be a big part of that, sometimes you will hurt one another or offend but to create the strong bonds necessary to overcome space and time there must be nothing too great to keep them apart. When you put all your egos aside and focus on the foundation of love that brought you together you understand deep in your soul that love conquers all things and is the greatest power given to you.

Family can make you crazy, exasperated and frustrated at times but it is also the space where unconditional love, immense happiness, contentment, and a feeling of belonging are made and there is security when you feel a part of that. There is no family in this world that can accept the trophy of most perfect, there will be times when friction happens or someone isn't speaking to another member of the family and it can be a juggling act, keeping everyone happy and together.

When you are family you decide to love those people for always even if there may be times that you struggle to like each other, you never give up and you are always there to defend in times of need. Everyone needs a tribe to belong to, one that's intrinsically woven together by strong bonds that are difficult to break; it is by this very construction that fuses those relationships throughout your life.

Many men spend their life travelling the world in search of the best for their own but they already know that it doesn't really matter where they settle, for the true value of what they own is within the very creation of that which they have built. Love those closest to you, if you're hurting find a way to build the bridge necessary for you all to heal and *Choose to Climb*.

Quote

"Cherish your family, they are priceless gifts you have been given to share your life with, look after them always."

Geraldine Mair

Affirmation

I love my family, I am so grateful to have them in my life I will cherish them always. I am a great Mother/Father and I teach my children through love how cherished they are, giving them a safe place to grow.

Strategy

Too many families become disjointed or estranged, separated from one another through a desire to be right. Stubbornness and ego can affect family units for decades.

1. Always choose to right a wrong as quickly as possible or you run the risk of it developing into an open wound that cannot heal, or a canyon so deep it becomes impossible to cross.
2. Never be too proud to apologise and make amends. Life is so short, choose to look past the shortcomings of others, there can never be any winners in this kind of battle as both sides always end up on the losing team.
3. Be the one that heals the rifts don't look to score points. Your family know you better than anyone else; give yourself a life full of love and memories that can only be enjoyed when everyone is willing to overcome any hurdles and stay together.
4. Always remember that it is better to be kind than to be right.

45. Have You Ever Messed Up

Every single person has messed up at some point in time, and guess what, you're probably going to do it a whole lot more as you grow and learn new things. If this happens don't beat yourself up for it or get exasperated, there is a real risk within your mind towards giving up when you adopt this stance, you will talk yourself out of taking the necessary actions needed to get you past the impediment, and then spend endless amounts of time trying to justify the decisions you made to stop.

You were not born to fail, crushed beneath problems that you think you are too weak to face, you can overcome anything that is placed on your path, and an unyielding drive will push you to find answers to any test. When you fall, get right back up and keep on moving forward, life can be taxing, it can make you question *Why Me!* What have I done to deserve this! The answer is nothing, no one is out to get you, and no one is operating some awful scheme to make sure you end up on your knees. You must refuse to allow any mistake to ruin a beautiful life. You are fully responsible for your own reality and you have the competence to alter anything about it that no longer serves you well, once you learn to become aware of it you possess the power to alter its route and facing a new day becomes a lot less scary.

Let go of all the worrying as this can often make a problem a lot worse, simply by the attention and energy you are giving to it, remember to always listen to that inner critic, the one that keeps you in uncomfortable places a lot longer that you should be prepared to stay there. Never keep a score of your errors as this will only serve to cement a belief system that will create much more of the same in your reality.

Life is a journey and can be fraught with hurdles but with lift and speed you create the momentum that allows you to sail right over the top to the other side where you can look back and see you achieved that which you believed could not be done. *Never Give Up!*

Quote

"You are human and by this very fact you are flawed, you may fear but you are strong, you may falter but you are resilient, you may fall but you are equipped with the capacity to rise."

Derek Mair

Affirmation

I forgive myself for any mistakes that I have made, I choose consciously to no longer dwell on any subject or event that continues to pull me in the opposing direction that I am aiming for. I am a competent individual and I can start again with a different outlook. I am a winner.

Strategy

By asking better questions of yourself, going through trials allows you to search your subconscious for a solution, when the noise in your head is too loud it drowns out any answer that may be there.

1. Fight for that which you believe to be right and true, hold yourself to account in every action that you take or any mistake that you have made.
2. Be responsible and take ownership, integrity is everything in relationships and failing to do so can play havoc in your day-to-day life.
3. This in turn gives you the ability to get past the problem and come out fighting to overcome.

46. Living With Children

There will be many days that your children, regardless of age will test the boundaries of the household. Not one comes with a "how to" manual, but each child deserves a foundation of love. To keep them safe you should offer them a few things that every child needs, whether they realise it or not. Boundaries and discipline are a must for any child, contrary to some people's beliefs, they think that allowing unlimited freedom is the best approach; they try to be their child's best friend first before they are their parent. If you apply this to a child's thinking they will question in their own heads the reason for it. They may think it's great initially, no rules to adhere to, no curfew, no accountability but they may also question why you would allow it, you might think you're a cool parent, very modern and forward thinking. You would be wrong. Children need love, guidance, and a listening ear to help with any issues they may be going through.

Allowing them to do as they wish, whenever they want runs the risk of influence by others, mixing with the wrong crowd, becoming the targets of those who enjoy participating in abuse of those they perceive to be weaker than them. Although there will be exceptions to every rule, teaching them a level of respect for themselves and others is critical in their development, knowing where they are and who they are with should be non-negotiable and insisted upon.

Protect their rights, instil self-worth, but keep them safe to prepare them for a life independent of mum and dad. This approach offers the best grounding for this generation to then go on to influence the next one. Lead by example and when your children are grown and able to make their own decisions in life they will indeed be your equal and at this point hopefully your friend too.

Choose To Climb

Quote

"There is no greater gift in this world than the gift of a child and there is no greater responsibility for that reward than to administer direction and unconditional love."

Geraldine Mair

Affirmation

I love my children and the way they enhance our family. I am a confident and competent parent always choosing to impart sound knowledge and a safe space for my child to express him or herself. I have been blessed with a family to raise, I realise the gravitas of this responsibility and I am able for the task.

Strategy

Talk to your children often; encourage them to participate in the family. Limit times spent on media devices, phones, game consoles and the like. Make family time an important part of your daily routine, your children are very receptive and if neglected it can sometimes cause them to get into trouble just to gauge a reaction or get attention.

1. Have dinner with your family each night or when you can, make it a habit and use this platform to encourage open communication.
2. No one can be the perfect parent all the time, but make it a priority to provide a safe space that keeps them on the right path.
3. Teach them to embrace the differences in others, show them the beauty of friendship in the way you treat each other in the home.
4. Give them a foundation that they can build upon without compromising their own values.
5. If they get into trouble help them by talking things through and explaining how to make better choices in the future. In my personal experience with our own son this has helped him to format his own opinions and develop a caring heart.

47. When You Feel like Quitting

If you have found yourself in a bad place and you are ready to give up, think again. Pain is a very temporary state and it doesn't last forever, nothing does and even though at the time it feels very real and you're only thought is to run, I urge you to reconsider.

When you feel like giving up stop and reflect on all the reasons that you choose a certain path in the first place, it's always better to digest all the evidence before you decide to quit, know the difference between giving in because you've had enough and giving up because you're too indolent to fight for it. If you have the heart of a quitter you will look for every reason and excuse not to start and you will find it. If you are weak in spirit you will start the process but with a very heavy heart, you will drag your feet and you will not have the determination or the willpower to see it through to its end.

One of the most common components that inevitably guarantee failure of any task is getting into the habit of giving up way too soon. If you don't see results you will either give up or move on rather rapidly to the next thing, not realising that to win the task you must keep on going, this takes courage and a will that never falters at the first barrier.

When you're ready to develop the spirit of a champion then there are a few things you need to know. You will have to be committed to the cause and find the strength necessary to plough through the thick of it to come out on top, because this kind of individual does not know how to quit.

Start now and make it your goal to attain and foster the attitude of a victor, you are stronger today than yesterday and you will be even more tomorrow if you stand firm in your conviction to finish. Remember the pain of the moment will pass but if you quit when you're almost there the regret can last forever. *Choose to Climb.*

Quote

"Self-discipline is the major ingredient for achievement, and achievement takes years."

Geraldine Mair

Affirmation

Today I embrace the heart of a person who chooses to climb, I refuse to give up or give in, I am more than capable of reaching new heights that I set for myself and I am ready to take the challenge on so I may see the results that I truly want for my life.

Strategy

If you are still trying to achieve your goal even if you have found yourself on your knees in the pursuit of it, you have not failed...

1. Make a commitment to finish what you start. Do whatever you have to, for as long as you have to do it, until you do it.
2. If things go wrong accept it, your errors will give you data to improve your approach the next time.
3. Quitting only leaves you with a feeling of failure further down the line, remember this when you start to think this way and keep going.
4. Your internal fears are always the markers that will make you question your own decisions, to overcome that dialogue; you will have to silence your own wayward thoughts that are driving you down the wrong path.
5. Your own feelings of accomplishment will give you cause for celebration when you can push beyond the barriers that have kept you in the same cyclical motion of defeat for too long.
6. When you know your capacity for completion and success you will never quit again.

48. Stepping Up

If you never go after the life that you want, you will never have it, when a different reality is longed for; something must change, if you don't shift from where you are you can only ever stay in the same position. Looking at alternative options will develop the necessary courage to create the vehicle to face your fears head on. Winners always keep moving and it's always forward.

Stop burying your head in the sand and hoping that by the next day all your worries will have magically disappeared. You were never designed to observe your life thorough the rear-view mirror, so stop looking over your shoulder you're not going that way. The only effective method through is with massive action, do not let events that have happened define you, it is not you.

The visions you create in your own thoughts have the capability to either propel you into a fantastic future or one that keeps you exactly where you are, frozen and unable to step up, or worse, in sinking sand that pulls you into its depths, where every moment becomes a fight to keep your head above the water. It's not enough to just stare aimlessly at the mountain in front of you, be ready to step onto that incline and go the distance.

When ownership is accepted in the minds of those who are willing your limitations will fall away, allowing a new response to surface, however the only way to grip that new reality is to stop resisting the changes that you need to embrace.

Stepping up confirms to yourself and others that you are equal to the test, your self-confidence will rise and your outlook will alter, if you want to experience all the gifts in this life then get prepared to do the work and pay the price, the reward is a whole new beginning, a better one.

Choose to Climb

Quote

"There will always be things to overcome, inside of you lies all the potential for combat, you were born great, all you have to do is open the lid to the possibilities that lie within."

Geraldine Mair

Affirmation

I am possible, I know that in taking ownership for all my decisions I give myself the chance to reach the success in my life that I was designed for, I am creative and know that when I seek a solution it can be found. I can overcome any hurdle and try again.

Strategy

It's too easy to continue to look into the past to find solutions for issues that you face in the present; the danger in doing this is that you may end up with the same situation over again if no lessons have been learnt. The answers will never be behind you; life is in constant motion but always moving forwards never in reverse.

1. Learn from life's foibles and continue to grow through the development of yourself.
2. Participate in this constantly changing universe, always keep your focus in the now and be ready to jump any hurdles on your path.
3. Push yourself to do just one thing that frightens or scares you a little, for when you face your fears a stronger version of you emerges, letting you release any past pains that are hampering your growth.

49. Dealing With Addictions

Understand that when you meet a person who is addicted to any substance, it is not the drugs or the alcohol that makes them the addict. It is the daily pain that drives them to escape from a tortured past that they have not been able to rationalise or overcome.

In the beginning it will be a euphoric state that they continue to chase after but as the intensity of this state diminishes and they are in its clutches the goal from here on in will be to avoid the pain, the pain of going without.

No one wakes up one day and decides that they are going to take this destructive path, for many it happens over a long time. Once in the grip of addiction it becomes your friend, it takes you to a place that you can forget all your woes, it enables you to escape your own reality but at the same time when you find yourself devoid of the substance, it becomes even more difficult to cope when reality recaptures you. Some of those lost souls who enter down this path do so because they have very little to motivate them towards a better direction.

Even those who manage to overcome their demons and push through to the other side will always have to stand guard at the doors of their mind. Given the correct conditions or a strong influence it can be a temptation that even they may find too great to resist. When a mind that has been poisoned and temptation rears its head again, their old addictions if fed can bloom once more pulling them back into an abyss.

Addictions of any kind are very hard to control when you are in the clutches of something more powerful than your own will. It takes only two things to persuade an addict to continue down their pained path. Give them whatever it is that they crave and cannot cope without, or make threats to deny them their substance of choice. This has been happening for years with individuals who control the markets all over the world and those unfortunate enough to fall into the net. Before anyone can free themselves from their hell, they alone must realise they have incarcerated themselves into a prison they hold the keys for. Refrain from judging what you do not understand its helps no one and has no impact on the problem at large.

Quote

"Understand that those who are addicted to any substance are totally powerless until they identify and find the emotional need they are trying to replace elsewhere and regain the power to defeat it."

Geraldine Mair

Affirmation

I am a conqueror, I can overcome what is keeping me in its clutches, I can seek the help that I need, I am whole, I am good enough, I deserve a life full of joy and happiness.

Strategy

We are in the grip of an epidemic where dabbling in recreational drugs appear to be the norm, especially in the nightclub scene. There is no reason that you should ever want or need to put these things into your body and mixing it with alcohol is a dangerous recipe that could extinguish your life.

1. If you are an addict or you have dabbled due to peer pressure and you are worried about your future and the way it is making you feel, act now.
2. Speak to a friend, a parent, a neutral party experienced in this field that can get you the help you need before it spirals into a situation you have no control over.
3. There is a way out, realising that there is an issue and owning up to it is the first positive step you can take.
4. The reality moving forward is that you may have to remove some people from your life that continue to tempt you. Staying on this path will be bleak or worse it could be fatal.
5. Life is magical, there is so much to experience and the euphoria from these moments will be much higher than anything you could put into your body. Don't be the one who misses the journey because you thought you had found something better. Unlike the first choice it has no longevity or future.

50. The Power of Giving

There is much to be said about the person who gives wholeheartedly with no expectation of return. But it is not so much what you give but in how much of your own love that you put into that act.

Lightening another's burdens through giving is indeed the most selfless act there is. It's so easy to get wrapped up in your own importance or self-indulgence and the opportunity is missed because it's viewed as work, when you choose to build relationships with others everyone wins, if you're not giving your all and putting what you can into that union then you're wasting your contribution.

You can accumulate many material possessions and this will give a great life full of things, but real fulfilment will be yours in what you choose to give to others, not in what you get for yourself. It is indeed much more selfless to be a happy and helpful soul, it is a personal choice everyday but it takes energy and a willing heart to make it so.

People can take those who elicit these qualities for granted. Try not to, be grateful to have them around you and in your life, if you are looking for people to emulate, gravitate towards those positive giving friends, family and associates that lift you higher everyday with little effort. It only takes a small group of people to want to make a difference and change their surroundings by engaging in the act of giving; in this life it's probably the only thing that ever really has.

The selfless giving of oneself to others represents the value of one's true wealth, if you are a rare example of someone who dares to reach into the darkness of another's fears to pull them into the light then you are worth more than any prize. You are an incredible person and a perfect illustration of someone who always *chooses to climb*.

Quote

"In this world the road to real wealth lies within all of us, it is in the gift of giving."

Geraldine Mair

Affirmation

I am love, I choose to give in a selfless way, I wish to be the best example that I can to others watching, I am compassionate and loving, I will help when I can and give freely of my time to others.

Strategy

It takes no time each day to adopt an attitude where you can pay it forward. There are many moments when the opportunity to help another will present itself.

1. In everyday life think of the many things that come up where you can assist someone else. Opening a door for a person in a wheelchair, helping an elderly person across a busy road. Babysitting for a friend to give them a well needed rest. These are only very few examples of an inexhaustible list of possibilities.
2. Be aware of what is happening around you and before long there will be numerous tasks that you can assist with.
3. Helping others inadvertently helps you too; it fills you with a sense of pride, a feeling of contribution and satisfaction just by participating.

51. Start Every Day with a Grateful Heart

Be grateful for all the amazing gifts you have every day, as soon as you wake and have the grace to acknowledge it. There are many people in this world who have far less than you but find a way to be grateful regardless. Finding contentment should be something that you don't have to look too hard for, yet there are still too many looking for problems or creating them when there are none, drowning in their own drama.

There is a culture of competition developing within society, a pre-set standard of more, better, richer, prettier, all of which are ego driven. You are very blessed to live in a time where so many things are at your disposal, yet you take so much of it for granted. This is a one-way ticket, no do-over's, no going back. This is a once in a lifetime opportunity for you to embrace it, all good and bad; there are no mistakes only lessons.

Try not to waste your time complaining about what you want, what you don't have or what you think you need in order for your life to feel complete, if you have a dream or a goal and it has the potential to enhance your life or the lives of others, go out there and get it.

When you have an open expression of gratitude in your life you hold within you the power to change everything in your world. Try to be flexible always, especially when you meet someone whose experiences in this life differ from your own, their battles may well have been challenging too and it's not your place to evaluate them.

Live a life full of passion and embrace each moment with expectation of what it will bring you. Go out with the intention always to leave those whom you meet better than how you found them. Instil hope into the hearts of those who have lost theirs and show them that human kindness is still thriving in our world today. Be kind, be bold, and be grateful. If the only words you ever say during your lifetime is "thank you" it will have been enough.

Quote

"It only takes a moment to realise that the smallest of things in our life should make us truly grateful, when you live with the utmost appreciation of all that is around you it expresses the best side of who you really are."

Geraldine Mair

Affirmation

I will rise each day with gratitude and possibility for all the wonder of the day ahead. I know that I am the first example to others of my inner resonance. I am the miracle, it starts with me.

Strategy

1. Look around you just where you are right now, look at the furniture if you are inside or marvel at the beauty of nature if you are outdoors and just think of the miracle that is in the creation of all things that you miss every single day because you are not living in the present moment.
2. The hands of another made the beautiful pieces that surround you in your home, borne from nothing more than an idea or dream that resided in someone's heart and brought to life with a desire to make it so.
3. Learn mindfulness, it brings you into the present and with it the appreciation for all that is.
4. Start to engage all of your senses by taking time out in nature to appreciate all that is. An elegant tree that began life as a tiny seed, a meandering river that has carved a path to the ocean over many years, all of it magical all of it miraculous, and all of it a part of your life experience what a phenomenon.

52. Skeletons in the Closet

Every single one of you has skeletons in your closets. Events from your past that you would prefer to forget given the choice. There are those you meet in life that can be very convincing, they hide their past mistakes behind a mask that they wear every day, and then engage in the judgment of others faults, ones they haven't managed to hide quite so successfully.

Some of you are just better at burying your secrets in the back of the wardrobe behind the coats and the shoes. Perhaps you should think before you speak, do you have a right to question another's actions even if it was wrong at the time, should you become the moral compass for everyone's decisions in life.

Surely, you are all capable of foibles, you all have the capacity to trip up sometimes unintentionally, perhaps you should learn to be tolerant and forgive those whose standards have slipped below your own. Remember while you're busy passing judgments on others, you run the risk of the door swinging open and all your own blunders falling out.

Just remember the only time that matters is the moment you are living in right now. The only reason to remember your mistakes is the lessons that came from them; these help you to grow beyond that mindset. Change is the only constant and giving energy to anything that you can no longer affect is a waste of your life. When you release your past mistakes that you tried to hide, you are accepting what's happened and choosing to move on. You make room for hope and opportunity to enter where before there was disapproval and condemnation.

In your humanness, you lose your balance from time to time, but there is no real merit in punishing yourself or others for it, your biggest mistake is holding onto anything that cannot be changed by carrying your past around in a suitcase with you. Hang it back up in the closet where it belongs forgive yourself completely and close the door it no longer serves you.

Quote

"The experiences from your past are where your memories reside, but they should be viewed as nothing more than a lesson or a teacher."

Geraldine Mair

Affirmation

I release my past and the pain associated to it. My errors cannot define my present; I let go of them now and any residual guilt. I am at peace with my decisions and I move forward with everything that it has taught me, knowing it has made me who I am now and I am grateful for the lessons.

Strategy

When you constantly go over errors that you made in the past you will always find disappointment.

1. If you have caused hurt to another or if someone has let you down or betrayed your trust, own it, repair any conflict where possible and move forward.
2. Find forgiveness in your heart for past hurts, regardless of who delivered them.
3. Forgive yourself for your own faults, you did what you knew how to in that moment so let it go.
4. Forgive your enemy and refuse to allow toxic thoughts of that person to mar your days and let it go.
5. Forgive a family member or friend who let you down for whatever reason for in doing so you can let it go.
6. Get excited again because your focus is now forward thinking and expectant, each day from this point can be full of possibility if you open the door and allow it in.

53. Engaging in Negative Self Talk

Every day your actions are predetermined by the scenarios that you play out in your mind. Negative people will and do talk themselves out of everything during the day, things that they are fearful of, threatened by or too lazy to engage with and then make excuses to themselves and others to justify their actions. If any of these sounds familiar to you then you need to stop! You are making yourself into a victim instead of a victor. No one enjoys being around someone who is always bringing the tone of the conversation down, you can only play that card for so long, eventually though you will find yourself alone as your actions and approach will have alienated those that you claim to care about.

There is no one out there that is better or more capable than anyone else, only the internal stories that you tell yourself make it so. You need to develop a stronger drive, an ability to go over, under, around or through any obstacle that gets in your way and an obsession to never give up on any dreams that you hold in your heart.

It takes practice to hone these kinds of personal skills, but you are all capable of it. Stop telling yourself it's because you don't have the money, you don't have the education, or you don't come from the right area. These are all excuses that will continue to prevent you from reaching your own personal summit. It starts with belief in yourself and a knowing that you deserve it, once you reach this point everything just clicks into place.

When you spend too much time inside your own head convincing yourself how bad thing are or might get, remember that you are always listening to this script. If you have been criticizing yourself for years and you still don't see the results you've been striving for, would *now* be a good time to approve who you are instead and see what happens. Never stop learning and improving yourself. Knowledge will only take you so far but the application of what you learn can take you everywhere. *Choose to Climb*

Quote

"Those of us whose glass is always half empty will never be able to see the world through the colourful lenses that others wear unless they choose to come out of the darkness and into the realms of possibility."

Geraldine Mair

Affirmation

Today is the first day that I decide to make a change to my internal dialogue, I realise that if I am committed to seeing a different reality than the one I am currently experiencing, change is paramount and I will begin the process now!

Strategy

If you are a person who spends a lot of time telling yourself that you will never amount to much, then you have made a conscious decision to settle for less that you deserve. It takes discipline, determination and a desire to want to change your current situation.

1. If you feel that you are a negative individual and it is bringing you down or pushing others away then it begins with you. Start a gratitude journal. Write something positive that you are thankful for in your life every single day. This reprograms the subconscious mind to see things in your own reality in a more positive way. You will focus more on all the blessings in your life instead of things to constantly complain about.
2. Being positive is far more likely to attract those whom you wish to befriend, the alternative is that you will continue to repel.
3. Think before you speak.

54. The F Word

Faith is a source of strength that continues to show up in your life if you continue to look for it and expect it. Faith cultivates expectation of the best and allows things to happen. It is the replacement for fear; if you choose to engage this power with a fearless heart real miracles are possible.

If you are frightened and worried all the time you will never be in a position to face your doubts, if you continue to expect the worst as some kind of punishment or retribution for all the mistakes you've made, it can keep you from your true potential for a whole lifetime, because you believed yourself to be incapable of reaching beyond the limits you had pre-set.

When you replace fear with love, you become immersed not in darkness but in beautiful light, for all of the possibilities. Faith doesn't involve believing in a far-reaching future it is in the *NOW!* What life will bring you today? Become an optimist, this is what leads to the greatest of achievements, without it nothing can be done, the challenges in this life are not usually what holds you down it is your inability to see you own strength and the excuses you use towards taking any action, this keeps you trapped, settling for something less than you know you can be.

Faith isn't necessarily solely based in religion although that is the most common reference for it. It comes from something deep inside, a knowing that it will all work out even when evidence of it cannot be seen.

Having faith is a gift that you all possess and can harness at any moment. It is your own hesitation that's creating all the problems you are manifesting into your reality. Believing in the best is a choice and the greatest miracle of free will. Connect with this invisible power and know that when you come from this podium it has the power to connect you to the source that can move mountains.

Choose to Climb

Quote

"Fear is nothing more that the absence of faith; Faith is nothing more than the acceptance of a better possibility."

Derek Mair

Affirmation

I believe in myself, I believe in the best outcome. I know that with faith there is hope and with hope there is everything. I have within me the potential to create the life that I wish and with faith that probability rises.

Strategy

Faith is described in the dictionary as the complete trust or confidence in someone or something, with no physical evidence to support that trust.

1. There will be times in your life that this will be the only thing that you have and you need to believe that the outcome will be a good one.
2. It can be scary when you have no physical evidence towards the outcome of a situation as it tests your resolve even when the road you are on seems uncertain. Do it anyway.
3. When you have faith for any action that you undertake it might not make the task easier, but what it will do is make it possible.
4. Always expect the best outcome even when you are fearful that the opposite may appear, most of what you concern yourself with often never materialises and you will have lost a lot of your time giving unnecessary energy towards it.
5. Always choose to step out in faith after all what does the alternative really offer you but a life full of doubt and worry that indefinitely produces more of the same.

55. Love and Fear

Here lie the two fundamental words that describe growth and paralysis. Fear makes you afraid and you pull back from experiencing all the wonders life can offer, but when you have love and certainty you become open to the possibility of amplification.

Fear is an emotion that can thwart change, although no one has a crystal ball to predict what may lie ahead for you. When you refuse to be held back by your own programming you can experience so much. Taking the chance to allow it in can sometimes feel like you are flying with no runway in sight and nowhere to land, this sense of uncertainty can breed fear into the hearts of many who need a definite path in which to aim for.

When fear takes a grip, it leads you into the false expectation that there's something placing you in imminent danger. When you feel this emotion be sure to ask yourself if it is just a response based on limited beliefs or are you at risk? The two are very different but the internal feeling can be the same, this is the primary reason that you talk yourself out of trying something or participating in anything new. The real fear isn't injury, its change because it makes you uncomfortable to reach into the unknown.

You can be safe and content at home, but that was never the point of life, true expression comes from the participation in all of it. The potential for increase and expansion lives in the hearts of the fearless. Push fear aside and replace it with love for your life, this opens all the paths to opportunity giving you the platform to fully create. Take a leap of faith with love in your heart, you can soar, spread your wings and know that the wind will carry you to the correct destination.

Quote

"When you choose to grow beyond your own comfort zone you realise in this moment that love has championed over your fear."

Geraldine Mair

Affirmation

I will no longer stay in the background or be happy to be a wallflower fading into the distance, I stand tall knowing that I am brave, I am courageous, I am capable and I have victory over any fear. I embrace change knowing it can bring only good things into my experience.

Strategy

There are only ever two forces in this life that motivates your actions, they are love and fear. When fear is your predominant drive you only have one choice, to disengage. This massively hampers your opportunities in life to make any real difference to your own or to anyone else's.

1. Step into your courage and start looking for opportunities to share love, start new friendships or travel to somewhere new that you never would have considered.
2. Love yourself enough to address any fear you have through the correct help lines to give you a chance to really maximise your life.
3. When you overcome anything, it gives you a sense of pride that you pushed though, courage and confidence is grown and you diminish the same event from holding you back again.
4. Never allow fear to stop you from enjoying or participating in anything. When you face fear you realise that is was never as scary as you thought, alternatively it can make you feel more alive than you ever believed possible.

56. Creating Your Life Path

You don't need to continue everyday along the same trail you have created. Convention zaps you of your energy and vigour, it gives you very little to look forward to and can lead you to a place you are painfully unhappy in because your zest and joy for life has gone and you feel as though you are living in Groundhog Day. I never understood the term comfort zone, as most of the people that I spoke to that made any kind of reference to it didn't appear to be that comfortable.

You will never change anything in your life until you change something daily, from here momentum is made and excitement begins. Surely, it's better to keep on searching for higher, a purpose that fulfils your needs, and something that sets the fire alight once more. Routine is the mother of all disappointments. However, the flip side of this is uncertainty and spontaneity that make you feel alive with excitement and anticipation again.

It's too easy to fall into a rut in life where you never stretch yourself or push for something better than where you are or what you have. Continuing to learn, builds real drive towards expectation and this comes with the conscious awareness that life is better when you live it this way. If you want to embrace a new journey and reach the potential you were designed for, then you better be prepared to walk the road less travelled, transform negative thought patterns into positive beliefs, and feel the power inside you grow because you're reaching for what excites you.

When life knocks you down and it will, get up and push even harder through the barriers, strive to find new things that you love and enjoy and begin to move in that direction. Pay very close attention to the messages that you receive in your own thoughts, those snippets of a life that you find yourself constantly drawn to. When you identify them, you will see that they are connected to your deepest passions and purpose for being here. Please embrace them with all the courage you can muster. Your enthusiasm will generate the energy required to ensure that from this point on nothing can stop you from creating your very own destiny path.

Quote

"The challenge most people perceive is the need to improve the world around them, without realising the key to doing so is to improve the world within them"

Derek Mair

Affirmation

I awake each day with excitement for what it will bring. I love my life, and I feel blessed, there is a limitless supply of wonder just waiting for me beyond my current place and I look forward with excitement and gratitude.

Strategy

When you become stagnant you become stuck without realising that you had the choice to change it in any given moment. You stay in your comfort zone because you think that there is nothing better for you outside of that box, this couldn't be farther from the truth. Nothing in this world is more fulfilling than a life full of wonder and expectation...

1. Stop settling for a life that is less than what you know you deserve to participate in. Will it involve doing things that frighten you? Possibly, but on the plus side you will feel a sense of aliveness that may have been missing for years.
2. Push beyond your boundaries, when an opportunity presents itself, grab it with both hands and enjoy the ride.
3. Don't stay anywhere that is unsettling you or that you dread every day you wake up. The only person that can change the direction you're going in is yourself.
4. Being rescued is not an option and exciting prospects will not fall magically into your lap. If you want a good life then do something about it. You can only ever be the person in the driving seat so take the wheel!

57. Enthusiasm

There are many things in life that can cause you to lose your enthusiasm. One of the main things is that you end up complacent, no longer appreciating what has been given to you and you are ungrateful. Blessings get taken for granted and hold no value so you stop noticing the importance of it. You become accustomed to all that you possess, forgetting the work and time it took to achieve it and you no longer show the gratitude that you should.

So many people are entrenched in worry, lack, jealousy, disappointment, and anger, unable to see dreams that were once there let alone make the changes to act towards realising them, losing your desire for better stops you recognising what your life has already given you and in doing so your enthusiasm for life is lost with it.

The lack of excitement in one's life can challenge you, wear you down and leave you at the mercy of it if you choose to accept that this is it. Reframing an uncomfortable time by imagining it as a stepping stone for you to reflect from, can help you to gain an alternative viewpoint and stop you comparing your life to another's. An inner strength can only develop when you get to a point that you are unwilling to go below, from here you can begin to climb again when something sparks your interest once more.

It's never too late to revolutionise your approach and get your enthusiasm for life ignited once more, but you must want it more than what you have right now, the pain of your current situation needs to be so uncomfortable for you to stay there that, you become compelled to resurrect the person that is no longer willing to settle. It can be your greatest asset when you allow it to surface again adding significance to all that you do.

Become someone with infinite passion it will lead you to open doors everywhere. Don't give up; don't stay in mediocrity when you were born to achieve so much more. Love your life and live it with *Enthusiasm*.

Quote

"As children our enthusiasm is endless, a waterfall of wonder for the world we inhabit. Don't give up these amazing qualities because you're an adult, keep it front and centre always."

Geraldine Mair

Affirmation

I am enthusiastic, I am encouraging, I have the potential to live a life of purpose, and I will be passionate and embrace the changes I wish to see in my life for I am already blessed beyond measure.

Strategy

1. Never compare your life to others who appear to have received a better deal, you are the only person that can modify where you are now, make a plan and get excited about it, you have just altered the trajectory of your day.
2. With every challenge you encounter face it with enthusiasm and a solution will be found.
3. Enthusiastic people find opportunities with everything they undertake, with a slight shift you can too.
4. You can only achieve a great result when you enter into things with enthusiasm; it's contagious and causes others to gravitate towards you ensuring continued growth in all fields of life. This can be you just choose this path.

58. The Need to Change and Evolve

In this life if you want to evolve then you must be prepared for change. The likelihood of a person who is incapable of making any kind of decision, will find it extremely difficult to alter their state of mind and therefore the direction their life may take.

You are all individuals and created to be that way. If you have the opportunity to meet people who are driven in the direction of expansion you will realise that they are the innovators, the inventors, the visionaries, it has always been that way and it always will. These are the people who see things differently, they are never confined by dogmas or doctrine of any kind and they understand the power of divergence to transform many things. You should have immense respect for those who refuse to conform; they are not prepared to compromise any of their core values and they will stay true to those morals in the face of every hardship.

So many people violate their own values but your internal compass will never make you feel truly comfortable with your choices. You can be swayed by the opinions of others and run with the pack if your only desire is to fit in, regardless of how it impacts your own life. But if you are ready to evolve into a brand-new reality your refusal to conform will leave you open to ridicule or objection, for the higher up the innovative scale you go the louder the voices will oppose you, just remember though change is challenging and it can be difficult to step out onto the ledge if you've never ventured there before.

Those who choose a different path are no more intelligent than you or I, but they have an obsession and drive that will continue to deliver the unexpected and all the things that others said couldn't be done. Celebrate your exclusivity and the gifts you bring to this life. You can't stop the future or rewind the past but small changes in attitude today can alter every tomorrow from here on in.

Quote

"You can choose to participate in change as a natural part of life, or you can choose not to... One thing is for sure the only way it flows is forward, so if you're opting out you better be prepared to be left behind."

Derek Mair

Affirmation

I invest time every day in the development of me. I love myself enough to understand that personal investment is priceless. I now set aside a chunk of space where I can inspire myself with material that delivers change and growth in all areas.

Strategy

You live in a fast-paced world connected globally now by the power of the internet and media. Be part of this exciting time by choosing to continue to educate yourself in something new each day. Even small incremental changes can have a massive impact on your life.

1. Commit to learn one new thing today and each day from this point on, it needn't be anything large or overwhelming but just one page of a book on a subject that interests you.
2. Any improvement in a forward direction can only change your life for the better compared to those who choose to stand still.
3. Change doesn't have to be a frightening thought; it can be the most exhilarating journey you could ever find yourself on, make a plan of action that you work through each day. Write down tasks you wish to achieve, get into action to see them realised by making them non-negotiable.

59. The Right Partnership

Are you making your relationship a lot harder that it really must be? Have you been making excuses for the lack of communication and affection? Have mind games become the norm, conversations been replaced with mobile phone messages, trust that's fading fast and hurting each other starts to feel ok for you? Do you believe the solution is to throw in the towel and scurry away from everything and everyone? You need to stop running and start dealing with the issues that are causing all the pain. Not one person has the capacity to fulfil every single one of your needs, so stop expecting them to. There is a deficit in each of us, our humanness makes it so, there will always be times when you slip up and disappoint one another, you have to get to the point where this is ok on both sides of the fence, where you accept the faults of each other and forgive whole heartedly, as choosing not to deeply harms the relationship.

Begin today to invest the time and make it a game changer, start to communicate, book nights out together, appreciate each other, learn to forgive shortcomings and really love the person that has enriched your life, before you lose sight of a future with them in it.

Decide there are no limits to the amazing life you can experience with your love by your side. Always keep interaction honest, open and clear. Don't tell lies to cover up for blunders, don't play foolish games with the hearts of those you care about unless you are prepared to pay the price, and the cost can be very high. You can be unaware of this until you lose the most precious pieces of your life.

When you show love in words supported by your actions sticking by each other becomes a privilege and not a life sentence. Be free to be an individual but be prepared to use teamwork when you need to pull together. Most importantly love each other in spite of your difference, that's what drew you together in the first place, learn to celebrate your union and be grateful to have someone special to share your life with, a privilege denied to many.

Quote

"If you remember what you loved in the beginning of the relationship and provide that platform of mutual respect for growth to continue then there need never be an end."

Geraldine Mair

Affirmation

I will invest all the necessary parts of myself into any relationship I am in or choose to enter, I realise that the only way to be truly successful is to accept the other person one hundred percent. We can grow together and create the environment for free communication without judgement; I commit to this and give my partner permission to do the same.

Strategy

It's too easy for any relationship to become stagnant over time when there is no investment into the development of it.

1. Write down ten things about each other that you have always loved, then go out for dinner or prepare dinner in your home, swap papers and make this the topic of conversation for the evening. This will help you to reflect on all the most important qualities of the person that you fell in love with, it should create quite a lot of memories for you both to reminisce over and hopefully a few laughs, reconnecting you at a deeper level.
2. Realise the uniqueness of your partner; disallow the small irritations so that real growth and investment into the future can become a priority once more.
3. If you do not nurture those whom you love don't be surprised if you turn around one day and notice they have left for greener pastures, or worse they have found what they deserved in someone else.

60. Expectations

When you waken tomorrow, why not believe just for that day that something wonderful is going to happen. No matter what you have been through or experienced make your new day the beginning of a mind shift.

Sometimes people mock those that try to be positive and see the best in any situation, stop, think for just a moment, why on earth would you choose the opposite, does anyone really think that their life will improve with an attitude that is negative and destructive to themselves or others?

No one is perfect and you are all capable of making mistakes and offending others but if you stop expecting people to be perfect, this changes your view of them and you can like them for who they are.

Expectation should not be based on anything from another person as this is the seed of suffering and the road to disillusionment, you cannot control others behaviours, but you can control the anticipation of each day being better than the last.

When you refuse help or assistance because of stubbornness or pride, you close all the doors to all the good in life. Don't think that if you look for nothing from others you'll never be displeased, unless isolation is your goal, it cannot lead the way to a better destination, nor can it enhance your existence in anyway.

When you have always chosen to come from negativity, you will always get more of the same in return, happy people make a conscious choice in any given situation, not because it's uncomplicated but with a good attitude it makes it easier to find a solution. Never be afraid to do what is right. Choose a life of expectation for what the day will bring and not based on the performance of anyone else. This causes an internal swing for opportunity to enter in; it changes how you view the world and the circumstances within it.

Quote

"Life should be a personal expectation for better with each new day by means of a positive attitude, but never one based on another's actions."

Geraldine Mair

Affirmation

I live with the constant expectation of the very best. I am open to new opportunities every single day. Events in my life grow my emotional muscles and make me who I am now.

Strategy

It's important to lead through example especially if you wish to hold others accountable when they disappoint you.

1. If you make a commitment to be in a specific place at a specific time or you promise to deliver on a certain task, then in order to have integrity you must hold yourself accountable to carry this through. When you fail to do so it puts your trust into question and others will not feel comfortable placing responsibility into your hands.
2. With each new person or relationship that you encounter, make it your goal not to prejudge until you have taken the time to get to know them properly. If they let you down at some point know that you have the right to call them out on it, but don't rely too heavily on others as their expectation can be very different from your own. This should be used as an indication of who you can and cannot trust in the future.
3. Live with expectation of the best always from life and in time this will indeed become your reality.

61. Seeing the Miracles

There are really only a couple of ways for a person to see their life through their own eyes, imagine that there are no miracles and everything happens by chance or imagine that every blessing in life is one. There are many beautiful miracles every single day; if you look you will see them all around you. The creation of life is a miracle. The beauty of nature is miraculous. The love you give and receive that's its own miracle right there. Anything that lifts another person higher is indeed a miracle and if you stop for a second and appreciate all you have no matter how small you will see the blessings in your own life.

Honestly, few of you are aware or realise you're in the midst of the extraordinary. There are so many people that have very little but still find the time to have gratitude and thanks for where they are in their life's journey. They understand that happiness comes from the inside and never from an external source. If you are always striving to fill an emotional void with material possessions it will only give you a euphoric feeling for a few hours or days, but it passes and your left once more deflated and searching once again for something to validate you.

When you remember to live in the now and draw your happiness from those around you who share your days, real enjoyment becomes your normal state of being. You become content and happy making memories instead of filling shelves with things that clutter your mind and your life. Whenever you recall a memory that has real emotional feeling attached to it, it remains active in your thoughts giving a wonderful recollection of a time to remember over and over again that lasts.

Become filled with wonder, gratitude, purpose, enjoyment, and satisfaction for another day to be here, then the scales will tip and you will have real balance in your life every single moment. Open your eyes with thanks every morning; you need not look very far for your own miracle because *YOU* are one.

Quote

"There are miracles in every moment in this life; they are in every breath you take, every beautiful moment you get to experience and an opportunity to participate in all of it."

Geraldine Mair

Affirmation

I am grateful for all that I have in my life. I choose everyday to make a difference and appreciate all the opportunities given to me. I am my own miracle and I remember what a privilege it is to be able to express that presence in the here and now.

Strategy

So much of your lives are spend always rushing around trying to fit everything in, leaving you stressed and out of balance. Put processes in place it releases time that ensures your days become a pleasure instead of a burden.

1. Organize your days to achieve more in less time. Mastering this can give you a lot more time to spend with your children, your spouse and your friends so you can really get into the flow of life and enjoy the miracles.
2. If you are always finding reasons to complain stop it now. You will miss all manner of wonderful things achieving nothing but the ability to rattle through life missing it all.
3. Implement this into your life starting today, clear out anything that you don't need in your home, including what's inside your head and get organised with your daily tasks. Once the clutter is gone and the horizon is clear, you will see the miracles in everything and really start to enjoy life again.

62. Showing Your Love

Do you still take the time to appreciate that special someone or have you let that side of your relationship slide? It can be difficult to keep things fresh and exciting especially if you've been together for many years, but investing in each other is what really deepens the connection of two people.

It's inevitable that life can just get in the way; careers, commitments, family and events can take you away from apportioning enough to the one thing that was non-negotiable in the beginning. It's a mistake on the part of many that pay no attention to this demise and then often find out after the fact when it's way too late to repair the damage. When you look around beyond your own importance and see that the familiar face is no longer there and has moved on to another place or person, tired of playing the waiting game and sickened by the repetitions of asking you to notice them, you become the recipient of a very difficult lesson.

If you are involved with someone and you feel that friction is creeping into the mix then you need to do something to stop it from sliding into a deep hole. If you promise to try harder then make sure that you aren't just giving it lip service, you will only be able to fool others for so long including yourself. There is no room for love to thrive when honesty and integrity slip so far down the scale of importance that it's no longer of any consequence to you.

You don't have to go to enormous expense either; the smallest of gestures can speak the loudest of volumes. Have a meal together, buy some pretty flowers, and run a bath; just do something out of the ordinary, showing genuine appreciation never goes unnoticed. But if you really want to create maximum impact and a foundation for lasting love then start making each other a priority every day. When you commit to become the other half of a couple and you promise to devote the necessary time to grow that union into a partnership that can survive the test of time, you need to fully embrace the level of that obligation and be prepared to do whatever it takes to make it through.

Quote

"Be sure that when you tell someone that you're in love with them, you are prepared to fully embrace the responsibility of that action."

Geraldine Mair

Affirmation

I will always bring my best into any situation, I will love openly and honestly knowing it is the best way to give my authentic self to any person. I am prepared to accept that I can love again even if I have been hurt in the past; I know that I am a great partner to the right partner and I am open to inviting it in.

Strategy

When loving a person and wishing to enter into a partnership for a lifetime it's important that you are sure it's the right decision for you and for them.

1. Don't play with people's feelings with the intention of scoring a point.
2. Never tell anyone exaggerated statements about what they mean to you if your goal is to get them to engage with situations that they are not fully ready for.
3. Take care of another person's heart it is a very precious thing and can be easily damaged.
4. If you have made errors correct them as soon as you can, take ownership for your shortcomings and be accountable it will protect your honour.
5. When you are genuine and caring there can never be any mistake that you have integrity and honesty, two of the most valuable attributed you can bring into any relationship

63. Live Your Life Your Way

Taking steps to make better future decisions based solely on your own values, means that you don't have to wallow in the suffering of it forever. It's ok to slip-up; you just need to learn from it. You can get lured into a life that was not designed by you. Getting caught up in the need for significance you become deceived by your insatiable need to impress those you don't really care about. The result of this decision can lead to enormous financial pain that you readily accepted and entered into. When you deny who you are in any given moment of life, you begin to conform and bow to the pressures of those who you believe are judging you.

Everyone dies but not everyone will truly live! Curtailed by their own fears and pressures placed upon them by ridiculous needs that were never necessary in the first place. Life shouldn't be about survival with the intention of arriving at the end destination in a wooden box, it should be about embracing all the amazing moments that make your story and your contribution a remarkable one. If you're aiming for a spectacular life then make it your purpose to leave an imprint, people won't always remember what you did, but they can never forget how you made them feel. Leaving a memorable legacy that carries on long after your gone is something you should all be aiming for, by choosing to follow an authentic life, never in competition with others but always trying to be a better you than you were yesterday.

Let your life's work be one that is constantly evolving with an intention to enhance yourself and the lives of those around you. Making your own rules will take you down the path of self-actualization, you should never have to behave in a certain way or shore up anyone else's ideals, it's much more important for you to follow what feels right in your gut. When your life is at its end I hope in reflection you each get the chance to say with a smile on your face and every ounce of spirit that was given to you;

"I did it my way".

Make your life exceptional and *Choose To Climb!*

Quote

"There can only ever be one person that you can measure yourself against in the pursuit of success, that person is you!"

Geraldine Mair

Affirmation

I am enough just as I am, I will live my life my way, I have no need to be in competition with anyone else, I am grateful for what I do and I am happy for anyone who has greater success, I know that in time and with commitment I too can reach all the goals I have for my own life. I will always try everyday to be better than I was yesterday. Learning will become an enjoyable habit, I choose me.

Strategy

Living your life through the comparison of others will never bring you the life that you really want. Each of us has a desire and a dream that was put into our own hearts and minds and striving to get someone else's life because you think it's better than your own is pointless at best.

1. Envy, jealously and pride will only take you to a very dark place where joy can never reside. Refuse to go there.
2. Be happy for those around you that are having success, by all means admire them, but never try to be them.
3. Focus on your own talents and have gratitude for all that you have and where you are now. Our lives although similar are all lived through a very different lens and it can't be any other way.
4. Choose to invest in yourself with constant never-ending improvement; success will surely follow with this fail-safe recipe. With consistent action your life can change in a way you never imagined.

64. Anchored to Hope

Are you often disappointed by challenges you face when you had hoped for a different conclusion? You should not be prevented from reaching your best by a few barriers or hurdles, don't view these things as an excuse to give up, see them for what they actually are, a redirection to an alternative option.

Events in life can test you and leave you feeling stressed and exhausted, surely it shouldn't be this hard. It doesn't have to be, it all depends on how you frame it or allow it to affect you and you get to choose. There is capacity for hope in the most desperate of situations, when you drop your anchor it keeps you stable so you can achieve focus. The human fortitude is immense and has an inbuilt system that is designed to overcome your greatest trials.

Don't spoil all you have the capacity to become by losing faith in the journey and the work required to get you there. On reflection you will see that what you now have was once among the things you had only wished for. If you are without hope it is like a ship sailing without a target, what would be the point of even leaving the harbour, you're never going to reach your destination?

Just over the horizon are all your hopes and dreams, it only requires that you programme the correct coordinates into the system and you will get there. Anchor yourself to hope always and in the face of extreme hardship if the first word out of your mouth is "but what if" then you still have the capacity for optimism because you are searching for an another answer. Once you make this shift and you realise that this too shall pass then anything becomes possible in that moment. There is no such thing as defeat only lessons to be learned or a different approach to be taken. The solution is always there and once the smoke clears you will have the capacity to see it once again.

Quote

"When everything is tumbling all around you and a hand reaches into the mist to pull you back up, take it you have just received hope for a better tomorrow."

Geraldine Mair

Affirmation

Hope achieves the impossible; the power of hope is very real. I choose hope in life, as I now know that it will always be stronger than fear. I choose to climb.

Strategy

When you feel tested to your very limits, it's a natural response to wonder if happiness can ever take root again. Know that this can be a temporary glitch as long as you make a commitment to move beyond whatever is keeping you stuck.

1. Give yourself emotional permission to feel the pain of disappointment then allow it to pass and get back into the game.
2. When life doesn't quite work out as you hoped it might, draw strength and support from the love that is all around you, get professional help if you feel you need it if it is overwhelming you.
3. Don't wait too long or allow yourself to spiral into a place that you find it difficult to function from. When there is hope there is always help, you only have to ask and with the right approach your best days are still out in front of you.

65. Toxic Influencers

There will always be people in your experience who drain you of your joy; they can become so hypnotised with their own problems that it consumes them and everything they do. Once you allow a toxic influencer to penetrate your own thoughts you give them the green light to affect your life and manipulate your thoughts.

If you are in a position at work that is difficult to remove yourself from, use this time to your benefit and treat the toxic person as an emotional trainer, this can help you understand what you don't want until you find a way to change your circumstances. When you were born there was an infinite supply of bountiful good seeds inside of you, choose wisely who you allow to impress upon you ideas that do not serve your higher purpose, plant your seeds in rich soil, in places that enhance your true passions and purpose.

Negative people will question your value, attack your image, destroy your credibility, trash your dreams and disbelieve your ideas and imagination. Hanging around with people who emit these qualities will leave you feeling worthless until you take control of your life and re-locate your friendships to a better place where the outlook is a more positive one.

Toxic relationships of any kind romantic or otherwise not only have the capacity to make you very unhappy, they have the potential to corrupt your own attitude towards others and towards life in general. If you let them in they will undermine your true nature and poison you to the point that will prevent you from realising how much better your life could be, if they weren't in it. Be very careful who you're connecting with and letting into your circle for they have the potential to raise you higher or pull you deep into a pit of emotional chaos that may be very difficult to free yourself from. It's not your job to fix others but it is your responsibility to take ownership for what you let into your space. *Choose to Climb*

Quote

"No person that is a toxic influencer will take the time to offer you any apology or explanation for who they are or any action they make, remember that you always have the power to heal yourself without their participation. Just move away."

Geraldine Mair

Affirmation

I give myself permission to be happy; I deserve respect. I will be the first example of how others should treat me. I move away from all that hurts or distresses me and I take total ownership for my happiness. I will not judge or condemn as I do not understand their journey, it simply does not resonate with my self-worth.

Strategy

If you are in a relationship with a toxic person you will already know. Your life will be a constant battle of living in fear; you will compromise your own desires, wants and dreams because toxic influences make it all about them all the time. This is a form of emotional abuse.

1. Assess your life if this is you; have you become completely closed down to the possibility of anything ever getting any better? Ask yourself how this relationship is enriching your experience.
2. It's not your job to fix others, so stop taking responsibility for their actions, they are responsible for themselves, do not get into a situation that you feel trapped by their manipulations.
3. Happiness is a choice always and no one person has the right to deny you that, to satisfy their own selfish needs.
4. Enabling their destructive behaviours only keeps you in your own punishing limbo until you choose to break free.
5. Choose happiness, choose a life of joy. Know that you deserve better and move away from them before they change who you are into something that serves them better.

66. The Right Kind of Personality

There may be times that you will have opportunities to protect the honour of others that will be worth the fight, or you may find one day that it could be yourself that needs to trust, allowing people to fight for you. If they disappoint you, walk away or turn their back on the relationship, don't waste time or energy trying to keep them around, when your life hits a bump in the road this is often when you get to see just how committed an individual was invested in protecting your wellbeing.

Do not try to effect or influence free will, work on changing yourself to become the best you that you can be and your world will then mirror those changes back to you in a positive way. Look for the best in all, but recognise that there will be times that some of those you meet will have to get off the train making space for seats to be occupied by new people, they're not meant to go with you to your destination so carry on without them.

Give yourself permission to let go of those who hurt you or who walked away when you needed them the most; never compromise your self-respect in order to satisfy another's objective. When you continue to chase after anyone who can't meet you half way just accept they are not meant to be in your story for the remainder of your journey.

There is a champion that lives within you, a fighter that is the best example to everyone you have the opportunity to touch, once you have developed this reputation, there will be many who will enjoy connecting to you on an individual level, and you will attract the kind of characters that admire your personality. Never compromise your internal worth to validate your own value for in time it will erode your nature. Choose to lead by example and everyone will want to follow.

Quote

"Remember in this life that people will gravitate towards attitudes, those that resonate with their own, make yours one that everyone wants to catch."

Geraldine Mair

Affirmation

I am my authentic self, I am proud to be me, I have many gifts and talents to show to the world, I am a great friend, I will always stay true to the person I know I am.

Strategy

A society of followers is being created desperate to fit into the space, the crowd, the team. Why do you do this? Why do you hide your true selves from the world? Perhaps you think that you have to conform to what society wants you to become, so that people will like you.

1. There is nothing in this world that is more attractive than a person who has individuality, integrity, truth, and charisma. Develop them.
2. Every one of you has these qualities it just depends on the degree with which you choose to let them rise to the surface or keep them buried deep inside.
3. Be yourself, be true to who you are, if you're loud be loud, if you're funny, be funny, if you're compassionate then be that, never hide who you are in any arena, it's exhausting to be something you're not and have to maintain that facade. Stop it!
4. Choose who you share your deepest dreams and your secrets with, not everyone is your cheerleader. Once you can identify your true essence you will no longer have to look to see who is on the side-lines, for the familiar faces that you can trust will always be there for you through thick and thin.

67. The Heart of Giving

When you see someone throughout the course of your life that is suffering, someone in genuine pain, be it physical or emotional, step up! Not because you have to, but because you want to make a difference in that moment and take away their hurt. Becoming wrapped up in your own needs and wants is the very thing that makes you numb to others who require love, understanding, affection, food, companionship or acceptance.

Walking around with blinkers on does not make the suffering vanish, it's still there, so stop judging others' lives, how they got there or how they ended up in a difficult situation. You are human at your very core and what emits from a warm heart is love and kindness, but when you refuse to notice the pain of others, you close down that empathic side of yourself, with the expectation that someone else will do it instead.

You will never truly have lived your life's purpose as a human being until you do something thoughtful for another who has no means to repay you for your kindness. Try to be more mindful as you go about your day. Look for opportunities that will be all around you, and never make another feel less than they are because you have the privilege of having more.

Give your love and compassion away, these are gifts you were given at birth that should be shared everyday of your life, do it for the joy of it, the grace of it, add to others instead of taking away the little dignity they have left. Always take care of yourself and your loved ones, but remember if you are well enough or capable to care for others who cross your path, then extend that quality. Be kind when you meet anyone that is fragile and suffering, in my experience most people are decent and friendly, but as a society you are taught to be overcautious. Try to be an example for others, take the time to show people how to express kindness; you are called to help when you can. Be the one who chooses a life without limits by setting an incredible example that others can follow and *Choose to Climb*.

Quote

"Realising that you are blessed enough to impact the life of another is the greatest gift that is available to us all."

Geraldine Mair

Affirmation

I am capable of showing empathy, I am generous and giving. I strive to have understanding towards those less fortunate than myself. I choose to be a positive example whenever I can.

Strategy

You will see many things throughout the course of your life here that will make you sad. The media and television show us the worst side of life every day. I hope that you will not harden yourselves to the misery that some endure every moment, but try to participate in the solution of it.

1. Make a difference to another person today, the smallest acts of kindness can be priceless to another in need.
2. Open doors to assist others.
3. Give a sandwich and a hot drink to a homeless person on the pavement.
4. Helping a family member through a difficult time in their life can be the catalyst that moves them beyond the obstacle and brings them back to their centre.
5. The act of giving lifts your very soul; it can have a profound effect on you. Do something wonderful for another person that you know can never repay your kindness, your life will never be the same.

68. Investing in Your Own Personal Development

Learning is the one true key to the expansion of your own awareness. Education is a very powerful tool in the hands of those willing to apply what has been learned. When things happen in your lives, treat it as an opportunity to take a different direction from the path you are on. Whatever memories you are challenged by from your past, do not have any power over you now unless you give attention to it still. See it as a lesson and do not let it prevent your own personal growth and then set about applying this principle to your life.

Education and achievement go hand in hand and you should always be moving towards this, yet a common mistake that a whole lot of you are making is that once your formal education is over, you settle into a life that is convenient and often repetitive, you stop pushing yourself to reach for higher or better. Desperate to be free of the shackles of studying it's easy to lose interest, but you stop learning new things and so you stop growing.

Commitment to your own improvement will show you that when you know how to do things differently, your armed with the ability to do things better. People will fear you if you have understanding, you are viewed as a threat because they will not be able to control you as easily as someone who is without it. You may be surprised by how far you can go when you know more today than you did yesterday.

Your personal growth is the finest quality you can offer to the world and becomes the vehicle for real transformation within the character that has a desire for change. Motivating yourself with positive material everyday has the power to elevate you into areas that you might not have otherwise considered? Once you have the knowledge in your grasp there is not a person in this world that can take it from you for it becomes the most precious fortune that you own.

Quote

"There is no real power in knowledge; only through the application of it can you create real change in this world, for otherwise it becomes no more than information."

Geraldine Mair

Affirmation

I am happy to learn new things. I am open to change and the opportunities that new learning's can bring into my life. I am constantly growing into a better version of myself every day.

Strategy

Stagnation will create no desire to improve and you will settle for staying where you are. Complaining about your situation becomes a pointless exercise if you are not willing to take action to alter that state.

1. Make a commitment to read one book a month in a subject that interests you.
2. Continue to try out new experiences that enrich your life.
3. Push your own boundaries that you have set yourself and never let fear prevent you from at least giving it a go. Once this happens it loses its power to immobilise and you gain wisdom that allows you to move beyond the problem.
4. Join a new group or evening class, it will offer you new learning's and connections to new friends you may never have met if you hadn't.

69. Healing Pain as a Group

Everyone can remember, if they were old enough, when Princess Diana was killed, or when the terrorist attacks of 9/11 in America unfolded across the news channels, you feel helpless, and horrified on a global scale. Even when you are not directly connected to the occurrence it's possible to feel immense loss on a combined level.

There is a side to these events that shows not only the very sad, painful parts for what has been lost, but also a very different side of the power of the human spirit, when tragedy hits this world people work together for the greater good of all. At this point there is no religious code, no racism, and there is no separation. In enormous tragedy there is a collective consciousness that surpasses all of the things that separate us daily.

The most important task is simply to save the life. People will place themselves in harm's way to move rubble with their bare hands, pull the injured from crushed vehicles or dig in landslides to find victims. Imagine if you could harness this level of compassion and apply it to all of your lives. Choose always to ascend to your highest and give freely of whatever gift you have to help. You should not have to wait until the most horrific tragedies like this catch you in their grip forcing you to relinquish your own needs for the life of another.

The true essence that lives in every human being can show a tiny glimpse of the empathic emotion that is alive in all of us. There will be chances in your lives where you will be given an opportunity to eliminate judgment that you feel and just do what you know in you very core to be right. Follow that call and answer it with every ounce of passion that you can muster. You can make a positive change to someone's life if you really want to. It may not be on a global scale but real inspiration begins in taking the first step towards a better world and you can start where you are with what you have, just one person at time.

Quote

"When you make a decision to make a difference no matter how small you start a chain reaction that can alter the future of our world."

Geraldine Mair

Affirmation

Change begins with me first, I am a loving person. When I hear the voices of need I will respond, I will always choose my highest calling for what I know to be right and true.

Strategy

How many times have you witnessed people passing by those in need who they perceive to be of less importance than themselves? Deciding how worthy a human being is based on your own limitation and perceptions is wrong.

1. If the only thing that you can learn in this life is to be kind to others then make a conscious choice to do that whenever you can.
2. When you see discord step up, do what you feel in your gut to be right, never put yourself into a situation of danger but if you can make a difference then do so.
3. Enter each new day with a new outlook and see beyond your own discomfort in order to feel the pain of another. Sometimes just an acknowledgment that you are aware of them can be enough to make them feel worthy.
4. Remove all your barriers created through religion, status and colour; the only outcome of this mindset is separation.

70. The Measure of a Man or a Woman

I feel it's important to move away from what you believe defines you as an individual. Each one of us has flair, the choice to contribute and the ability to express those gifts. It is wrong to think that your success, your worth, or your value is intrinsically linked to the personal accumulation of anything while you're here.

Ambition and knowledge are seeds for your life, and striving for a comfortable living is indeed your God given right and you are entitled to have a life that is full, happy, comfortable and abundant. Do not confuse fulfilling with someone whose only goal is to amass possessions believing that this is the only way their success can be calculated.

Our society tends to rate success on size, size of house, size of bank account, make and model of car etc. This is nothing more than a cultural belief that has created a social ladder that many feel is the only path to find credence, many that take this option are prepared to do so at any cost. There is little evidence to negate this belief and so many have created a very stressful existence in the pursuit of it as a measure of their worth.

A wealthy life is the foundation for all the most significant pillars in any individual and all must be equal to have balance and contentment therein. Relationships, financial security, significance, purpose, and love and connection are all of equivalent importance, so you see it can never only be about how much money you can acquire. If you make it that way you unconsciously sacrifice one of your other needs and this causes disharmony.

From this moment on possess the courage and the strength to walk away from anything that makes you feel less than you know yourself to be. Do not bow to the pressures of society and never place yourself into a position that you are living beyond your means to appease another. When your internal worth rises, meet it and allow it to shine right out of you like a beacon, the only things that you can attract from this point on are those that are worthy of you. Raise your bar and your standards with it.

Quote

"Remember that you are priceless and already enough, so never get caught in the trap of trying to keep up with others to protect your own ego, no one else has that power over you unless you give it to them."

Geraldine Mair

Affirmation

From this day forward, I will realise my true worth, I will protect that part of me refusing to believe that I am anything less. I am talented and honest; I will remove any need for competition to impress upon another, as this only degrades my own value

Strategy

Stop measuring your worth on the accumulation of stuff; never be embarrassed or ashamed that you do not have what they do in material terms or perceived intelligence. No one is more worthy than you and by escalating them upwards on the scale of importance; you are imprinting this idea into yourself all on your own. The value of a person can never be found in academic certification or money they acquire, but in the heart of the individual who has the capacity for love and kindness here is the core of true merit.

1. Treat anyone you meet from the waitress to the bank manager that organises your finances with respect.
2. The most important asset you have is your integrity. Use it! If you feel superior in anyway then it's time to hold up the mirror and change your approach setting a better example moving forward. In failing to do so you will continue to repel.
3. Never choose to be remembered for your arrogance, your obnoxious approach or your belittling attitude towards others; this will never gain you the respect of your peers or your friends if indeed you have any.

71. Words Are Seeds

How many times have you heard when you were growing up statements like? "We can't afford that" or "money doesn't grow on trees" or "you're not smart enough to do that". Be very careful what you allow to take root in your heart and mind for this is what your reality will reflect; it inadvertently places a glass ceiling on your potential to become anything more than what you believe you can achieve. What you record through your five senses that you allow to become your truth will inevitably turn up in your life.

This is your own internal programming that you are creating with each moment, a file on the standards you live your life by. It becomes a key indicator to the degree that you love yourself; your abilities, your talents, your skills and what you consider you are capable of.

What others say about you has the capacity to line up with your thoughts, when you plant seeds into your mind it's creative power in action, the more attention that you give to any particular subject the more you call it into your existence, you inevitably give it permission to show up. There is no benefit to constantly feed into the negative garbage just because you hear something about yourself does not mean you have to take it onboard.

Your words can be a blessing or they can be a curse depending on their content. Creating drama has the capacity to follow you around when you give it energy and consent, but change the words that you use and the way you frame them and everything changes. When you make a decision to live by poor standards, you unconsciously restrict your own growth, when this happens you hold within you the potential to do damage in others' lives that you influence. Know who you are, educate yourself on the power of your mind, remove the toxicity of things or other people whose values violate your own and live the life you were designed for, one without any limits. Only plant healthy rich content into your mind, with the knowledge that your harvest will then be a bountiful one.

Quote

"Words are seeds and seeds take root and have the capacity to form huge plants that become difficult to remove. Be careful what you place into the fertile soil of the mind unless you are willing to have it realised."

Geraldine Mair

Affirmation

I know that anything from my past or my upbringing can be changed, when something feels incongruent with my inner thoughts I will take positive action to change those paradigms and allow myself to choose a different path, one that I feel fits who I am now. I choose positive growth and I plant good thoughts into my mind knowing that it will produce a much healthier reward in the future. I am capable of change, I am creativity at work.

Strategy

Neuroscience teaches us that it takes thirty days minimum of repetitive action to create a new habit pattern, which then becomes our natural state.

1. Start learning about yourself and work on removing thought patterns that are affecting your self-worth it will show you what your real potential can be.
2. Set aside time everyday to work on yourself with books, tapes, meditation, exercise or music, something that lifts your feelings onto a higher plane and makes you feel alive.
3. Focus on a goal that shifts your emotions into a more positive arena and your capability for change becomes guaranteed.

72. Controlling Stress Responses

Where do you keep all of your trapped emotions from experiences that have deeply affected you in your past? All of the fears, anxieties and events that have created pains that are still ailing you with each new day; this will be your normality when you remain stuck in the very moment that it happened re-living it over and over again.

Every diseased pattern that you face in your bodies, whether it is emotional or physical, is caused by memories that are stored in your subconscious minds, when you trigger these you set in motion a pattern that affects you all over again as if it were happening right now, this is called the Maladaptive Stress Reaction. Learning to process your issues and get closure is so important if you are to release them from your grip. The real problem occurs though through repetition of these memories, our bodies go into reactive mode each time our thoughts stay focused in this area, leading to a chemical imbalance in the body that encourages all manner of maladies to manifest internally, keeping us in a diseased state.

Your body registers a continued emergency condition due to heightened emotions, this can cause anxiety and depression as the body almost goes into overload and inevitably has to shut down to cope, leaving a very low helpless state that can be difficult to recover from. Your life is such a precious gift and although many of us will go through unmentionable pain for whatever reason, staying locked inside your own internal prison only damages your life and those who choose to share it with you. It has the potential to fracture families, friendships and relationships.

Learning however to process problems, stresses, events or trauma in a constructive way, like talking to someone, finding a purpose that gives you joy, helping another person through your own experiences can all help towards getting the balance back. Empower yourself and allow healing at an internal cellular level to begin this will drive you upwards and forwards towards a happier, healthier you.

Quote

"There can be no pleasure in events of the past that brought us pain, releasing them gives us emotional permission to embrace the joy of life once more."

Geraldine Mair

Affirmation

I release my past and embrace a happier healthier future. It's ok to be happy. My best days are yet to come. I give myself emotional permission to move forward without any guilt but in the acceptance of joy in my heart.

Strategy

If you find yourself faced with a trauma or a tragedy that you feel you have to relentlessly punish yourself for, then please realise that the past has gone and mentally staying there is toxic. All of your habitual habits begin in the mind, regain control of the very thing that you have control over or you risk never getting out of the quick sand.

1. Get professional help to heal your pain so that you can participate in life again, staying in an indeterminate state where you're sinking will never take you beyond where you are or allow the highest or best version of yourself the space to emerge once more.
2. Change your physiology whenever you feel like this, do something, anything in that moment to focus your attention onto something that brings purpose back.
    Just move.
3. Give yourself permission to release that sack you are carrying and realise that in doing so your journey becomes a whole lot lighter.
4. Release any guilt of ghosts from your past they are not real only alive in the depths of your imagination. They will vanish into the distance when you allow it.

73. Asking Better Questions

Have you ever found yourself out of your depth or involved in a situation where you knew the only way from here was down. When you are focused on causing discord or you get a buzz from friction you are working from your ego and using manipulative tactics to attack another person, this is a lose, lose situation. Here are a few tips on avoiding conflict and hurt in any situation. When you are faced with a decision and someone has offended you ask yourself this.

Is what I am about to say going to hurt the other person it is being directed at? What is the desired outcome I wish to achieve here? Will this cause a terrible rift that will be hard to repair?

If you ask yourself these questions honestly and your answer is not a positive one then you need to reassess and come at it from a different angle. It's always a better result when you enter a discussion with the intention to diffuse it and find solutions.

Here are some better ways of reframing: How can I better understand why this person is so angry with me? How can I diffuse this situation and find a satisfactory compromise, where both people are happy with the outcome? How can I lead by example with a mature approach that removes any verbal confrontation?

Here is the answer to understanding one another in business or in personal relationships. These are only a few examples of what is possible but it gives a good overview of how you can change the perception of another, when you approach things from a different position. When confrontation arises in any situation and you end up screaming at each other the goal is lost and there will be no winners only pain and regret. Train your mind to be more empathetic in any conflict so that doors are opened to solutions and closed to anger. It is not a sign of weakness but of considerable strength and maturity. When you lose your peace, you lose your power. Game over.

Quote

"When you lose your peace, you lose your power and any hope of a solution in that moment."

Geraldine Mair

Affirmation

I will take the time when I feel threatened or frustrated to try to respond instead of reacting. I know that in doing so I create a safe space where solutions can be explored for a satisfactory end. I am in control. I always find a peaceful solution.

Strategy

Finding mature responses to any disagreements should be the only option that you are prepared to entertain. You would all do better at work, in families or in life if you take the time to find the space in the moment between reacting and responding. There is a massive difference in these two approaches and finding the right balance can make the world of difference.

1. Commit to remain calm in a heated situation and you will always remain in control of the moment.
2. Stay focused refusing to allow anyone to ruffle your feathers or push your buttons so that satisfactory negotiations can take place.
3. When faced with difficult moments in life take a deep breath before you speak with the intention of dispersing the conflict that is playing out.
4. When other parties feel they are being heard it often creates a platform where the whole event can be neutralised and a solution can be found with a better outcome for all.

74. Having Amazing Relationships

How can I receive unconditional love from my partner? It's really one of the most misunderstood things in the world, but the answer is simple. You must love yourself completely first. Don't look at your reflection and see flaws, don't speak words of failure or disapproval over yourself, this makes it difficult for you to be unconditional towards yourself or give the relationship your all. If you are continually worried that you're being judged, or measured by another person's standards you will never be able to truly let go of any reservations you have, drop your guard or surrender completely.

Desperation is a very unattractive feature and when you behave this way, it's very visible, there is a hole in you, a need that you believe another can fill but only one person can fill this void and that is yourself. No one outside of you can continually shore up this need and you shouldn't expect them to either, always needing validation and compliments to cement your significance to someone else, leaves you open to rejection where self-analysis and doubt creates a critical eye over your own character.

You cannot gain your self-worth through another's eyes; you have to recognise it in yourself first. The most attractive thing you can find in another person is their self-confidence, a knowing that they are comfortable with whom and what they are; this creates an irresistible attraction to that special person who can appreciate those qualities without any desire to change or erase them.

Don't chase love, love yourself and let it come to you through the qualities that you are emitting, love always gravitates towards love. Be thoughtful, be compassionate, be confident and be yourself. Relationships can only flourish where trust is the cornerstone and both parties are ready to execute that platform. Investing the necessary time in loving yourself first you grow confidence in the knowledge that you are enough, so when the time comes and you enter into a relationship with another person the flood gates will open and you will be ready to embrace that love with an open heart.

Quote

"Where there is attraction there is chemistry, where there is desperation there is nothing but the potential to repel."

Geraldine Mair

Affirmation

I will start where I am with what I have and I will begin to appreciate my true essence. When I see my reflection I will remember I am a miracle and age does not change that, it simply shows me what an amazing journey my life has been and the gift I've had to participate in all of it. I am confident, I am loved and I am enough.

Strategy

There is nothing in this world that is more attractive than a person who is confident in themselves, it radiates like a bright star in a dark sky and when they enter a room they lift the very vibration just by being there.

1. If you are invested in a relationship but you feel that you are repelling your partner through your own insecurities then work on your own self-confidence and worth in order to preserve the future of that unit.
2. Make sure you have interests of your own, taking time with friends or by yourself allow you to appreciate what you have without the need for constant attention all the time.
3. A healthy relationship is based on give and take along with some compromises, when it is heavily biased towards one or other there will eventually be discord.
4. The problem is never someone else it is always in your own behaviour and attitude when you have these traits, the solution can only be found in the development of yourself.

75. Let Compassion be Your Moral Compass

How many times have you walked along the city streets and seen a homeless person sitting on the pavement begging for a few spare coins? Do you look away to avoid what your eyes see, don't worry about treating them like you can't see them, they already feel invisible.

A human being is part of your whole world, yet you place so little importance on any kind of suffering that does not affect you. When you refuse to see the distress, you inadvertently become the one that sentences them as if they are guilty of some awful crime; you spend time trying to justify the reasons they came to be there, none of which are generally very complimentary, if indeed you give it any energy at all. As a nation why do we do this? Is it embarrassment? Is it disgust? Is it our egos getting in the way? Ask yourself these questions to find out where your own feelings lie towards this subject.

Could you dare to be the first person to extend a hand of hope? Dare to show compassion when no one else will. Dare to lead by example and show acceptance. You have the potential to be the one person that impacts their life in a way you know nothing about. You could lift their sense of self-worth to a higher place even if it's only in that instant.

Change can be small acts of kindness; an extension of friendship, a dream of a better tomorrow can all take place in a moment but only by stepping up and acting today. If you have a home, food on your table and people that love you then you are truly blessed my friend. Make today the day you choose to bless someone less fortunate than yourself with no expectation of reward.

It takes only one person to make the difference to another, when you push your ego to the side it gives an opportunity to come from a neutral place where there is no judgment only compassion and understanding, allowing our humanness to shine and acceptance to overcome all the barriers.

Quote

"Never let your surroundings or the voices of those around you direct your moral compass."

Geraldine Mair

Affirmation

I can help others; I will try to make a difference when I can. I choose to be a good example for my family, I am compassion at my core and I know that this is something that can happen to anyone perhaps even me, my life will be more fulfilled in the giving of myself.

Strategy

Never treat others that are less fortunate than you by your own standards. Their journey may have been different from your own but it does not give you the right to critique the outcomes of their decisions. Spend less time analysing situations and more time placing energy into finding solutions.

1. Although the passage opposite is based around homelessness, judgement comes in many guises. If you knew them would your attitude change, would your compassion kick into high gear? Think on this long and hard and decide never to judge again.
2. Remember how blessed you already are and try to find some level of understanding deep inside, this will help you move beyond your own conditioning even if it's only in the acknowledgment that you see them.
3. Losing your purpose can leave you feeling insignificant. Choose to give love, understanding and empathy and thank God that you don't have to find a safe place to lay your head every night where it's warm and dry.

76. Feeding Your Goals

When you decide to act on a specific goal, you must believe the strength of the conviction you placed beneath it when it was set. It's way too easy to get distracted by other things that stops you from reaching that aim. You will come across negative or critical people that you interact with daily, who never want you to succeed at anything or who constantly berate you for trying. These unhappy souls are the ones who complain and moan about the work that they do, they spend every minute just wishing for the time when they can clock out again, go home, or go on holiday just to get away from the grind! And they talk about it with anyone who is willing to give them air time. Why don't they take action to change it? Why are they prepared to spend eight hours of their lives every day being completely miserable?

You tend to find it's due to the fear of change, they worry about the risks but they take no action to address what they say they don't want, sadly though these are the ones who can't bear it when someone steps away from the routine to follow their dreams. These people are emotional vampires who have no ideas of their own, and no courage to follow through, stand guard and do not make the grave mistake of sharing your dreams with them, for they will tell you that you don't have what it takes to pursue yours.

There will always be people that are never going to be your biggest cheerleader and you're going to have to accept that this is the case. However, you can help yourself enormously by choosing who you share those thoughts with. It's always best in my opinion to keep these goals to yourself or to only share them with your partner or close friends that you know will be there to support your journey. Never be distracted by others negative energy, the fact that you are even setting a target, already places you head and shoulders above those who refuse to even try. Thinking negatively from the heart usually causes the mouth to follow, so try to see your goals like an overgrown hedge or shrub that requires pruning, when you prune anything it encourages stronger growth, so go after your goals and remove the cuttings (people) that are preventing your increase and push forward to your own summit.

Quote

"If you have a goal in this life to be better tomorrow than today, you have just accepted the gift you were given at birth, the desire towards increase, so follow that nudge, it was put there for a reason."

Geraldine Mair

Affirmation

I can achieve anything that I set my mind to; I am capable of expansion into better. I will keep pushing on, listening only to my own internal drivers, in doing so I understand any life goal I desire becomes a possibility.

Strategy

Setting goals are best achieved first thing in the morning, it helps to direct your focus and writing it down creates an anchor in the mind.

1. Get a notepad and each day write just five things that you would like to complete that day. Once you have clarity on this it makes it easier to concentrate on what actually needs to be addressed, rather than mindless tasks that are excellent at distracting you like email and facebook etc.
2. Make a point of only going into any kind of social media a couple of times a day to catch up with anything that is related to your tasks, this way it stops you from whittling away endless hours on things that simply do not merit your time or your energy.
3. Take the decision today, if you are living a mediocre life and you dread the alarm clock every day, only you can change you reality, so if you're really in a bad space take action today! And make all your tomorrows better, only you can.

77. Shooting For Your Summit

Decide to aim for better, continue to climb every single day, just tell yourself it's possible, this invites an opportunity to follow a different path to a happier destination. No one in this world finds themselves on the top of any mountain at any time, they had to work hard and climb their way over the obstacles to make it. Every single day they had to be consistent in their efforts to see their dreams realised. It's not an easy path but it is a rewarding one and the reason that you are here.

There is a formula to success in life, spend time in learning about yourself, read uplifting material that expands your awareness and gives you a different perspective of the world. Get around like-minded people who are in the business of sharing information with the intention of helping others. You are the sum total of those who you spend the most of your time with, make sure you are choosing wisely and you feel inclusive in their company instead of drained. If you are ready to change then you should expect to come across several roadblocks on the way, everyone must go through this, it will happen to you in different degrees, some will give up and slide back into the life they claim they are trying to escape from. But you, *YOU WON'T!*

When faced with any hurdle you must be ready to look at the options, if a particular approach hasn't worked in the past then the first thing you must be prepared to do is to change your mind. If you hit a wall get your climbing boots on and scale that obstacle till you can see the view from the top! Get into the game and work out how to get over it, the answer is always there to be found, but sometimes you need to be quiet enough to hear it, don't just turn around and give up, when you stumble and you will, make this your time to resurrect the fighter and try once more. Choose always to climb it's the only way to reach the summit and the view from that vantage point is spectacular.

Quote

"You will realise your internal strength has reached a new high when obstacles and failure only serve to act as the best motivation you have ever known."

Geraldine Mair

Affirmation

I am motivated for success. I know that anything is possible when I replace fear with unwavering faith. There is nothing so big that I cannot triumph over it. In reflection I realise how far I have already come.

Strategy

Personal development of you can be an inspiring journey, but it can also be a scary proposition if you have never questioned anything or always followed the crowds. There is real clarity and discovery to be found when you spend time investing into yourself on a consistent basis. When you do this, you open the doors to the most amazing possibilities.

1. Get around those who are motivated to climb, this will allow you to let go of any limiting beliefs that have been holding you back, it's difficult to cut ties with people you have spent a lot of your life with, but some of those that are on your path are not meant to be there for the whole journey.
2. Give yourself emotional permission to move on, it can sometimes be the most liberating action you can take.
3. Most of you already know who belongs in your life and who doesn't its only when you gain the courage to change the arrangement can you be truly free to soar to new heights. Never be afraid to release those binds from your life and follow a path that resonates with your internal moral compass better.

78. Love and Patience

Patience in any relationship is a necessary requirement to provide a foundation that can expand into real love and connection, both parties that are willing to endure will ultimately reach their goals, but like a harvest that takes time to gestate and grow, so does any union that is worth developing the patience for.

If you are stubborn or selfish, the chances are you are not yet ready to emotionally connect with that individual. In a loving relationship there should be no blame only deep and unconditional love. There are times when those bonds need space and time to become everything that they were meant to be, it is often in the timing that the desired response is achieved. Allowing equality by choosing not to force your opinions onto the other person creates the groundwork for an equal partnership, encouraging the growth of that character you fell in love with to thrive.

In so many people's experiences you find love in the most unusual places, it presents itself when you are ready to receive its wonderful gifts. You feel that instant connection that pushes you to find out more and you feel joined in your minds before that person has ever touched you with their hands.

Love awakens the soul to a higher calling, a longing to invest your time into something valuable beyond yourself and it plants the desire and drive inside of you with the anticipation that there is even better to come.

Patience and love throughout an enduring partnership that makes it beyond any personal challenge, will lead you to realise everything that should have broken you apart has created a stronger bond, in this moment you are a component of something so amazing that there will be nothing in this world capable of fracturing that foundation. If you reach this goal you have the greatest gift that money can never buy.

Quote

"You know that you have found your true home in life when it is no longer a building but has become a person."

Geraldine Mair

Affirmation

Every day I will choose to grow the relationship I am in or I am seeking into one of mutual respect, I give it space to flourish. I am patient when I need to be in order to provide a safe space for communication.

Strategy

Being open to new experiences can be difficult if you have suffered from rejection in the past. However, although it can be hard to overcome the hurt you mustn't tar all others with the same brush. There are many beautiful souls waiting for the opportunity to connect and make a life, be open to the possibility and you may just be looking into the eyes of your future.

1. Love can only flourish in a partnership that is equal and that never tries to mould the other person into the perfect image of what the other wants.
2. Always bring your authentic self into any union if you wish there to be respect on both sides of the relationship.
3. A real man will only ever wish to be true to one woman, he will love, respect and honour all that is you and in return you must offer the same conditions for your love to go the distance.
4. When there is discord and you face a test, be strong in your resolve, and if it is problematic fix it and move on.
5. If the hurt is life altering reassess your position, and think carefully whether this person deserves your love and commitment.

79. The Right Connection

There are many kinds of relationships, and there are different degrees of love that are shared within them. You can choose the level of attention that you are prepared to invest in another person but the best kind is one that has room to grow and change over time ripening and deepening in the process.

There can be no room in an equal partnership for an inflated ego, a need to be right all the time, one who constantly belittles or berates the other to make them feel superior in some way. You must always be prepared to apologise whenever you get it wrong or cause hurt, this doesn't necessarily mean that one person is right and the other is at fault, but a realisation that the relationship is greater than your own ego and therefore worth the fight.

Be wary of any man or woman that you engage with that seems more interested in moulding you into something that you're not, when it feels wrong it always is. Many strong individuals are worn down over time by controlling partners who are not prepared to work on their own insecurities but spend all of their time eroding away the strengths of the other to make them feel like the boss in the partnership, losing yourself in the process of winning the prize gets you no medal. It doesn't make you unintelligent for being in a bad relationship, it's possible to make terrible decisions in the name of love or because you thought they would change. You need to become the first example of how others should treat your heart.

You warrant the best, you deserve the respect, trust and commitment from your partner that you can build a future together, knowing that you are both equals on the same page. Someone who truly loves you will embrace all that you are the genuine article and would never need you to change. When there is a deep connection and an affiliation based on equality, patience and consideration, it can become the vehicle for the most amazing journey of two souls that are bound to grow through any struggle to an exceptional union.

Quote

"Finding love that holds your own values, worth's and dreams, is the universal answer to your own soul reflected in another."

Geraldine Mair

Affirmation

I am a great partner and I accept myself as I am, I acknowledge my partner as they are without the need or desire to change them. I will respect myself enough to recognise when a relationship is compromising my own internal values and I will reach for a higher standard for I know my worth.

Strategy

Nothing can be perfect all the time and life will continually throw stumbling blocks onto your path that you will have to find a way through together, in order to get the harmony back.

1. A good firm foundation where there is respect and love can weather any storm that comes its way.
2. If there are problems that no one is willing to find a solution to and it seems insurmountable or support is being withheld from you, then it's time to ask yourself if it's worth investing any more into a relationship that is giving you so little and eroding your self-worth.
3. If communication is an issue or you are frightened for the future, take a good look at what you have built before making any rash decisions. If you wish to save what is there and it is reciprocated then make the necessary investment by spending enough time together to correct any discord that has surfaced.
4. Create a safe space for both parties to talk though any worries so that a solutions can be found and you can move forward together into a brighter future where you can reconnect.

80. Are You Letting Your Fears Rule Your Life?

Do you want to make your mark on this world; are you ready to contribute with the objective of making a difference to benefit many? Are you stopping yourself from participating in that ambition or are you afraid to be different, to have a voice or to stand out in the crowd for what is right. Maybe you are worried that you will be judged, that there will be a chink in your armour, or possibly someone won't agree with your opinion, leaving you embarrassed and scrambling to defend yourself? Stop conforming to societies beliefs of what you think you should be; refuse to fit in with everyone else's idea of normal, what is that anyway? Why do you choose to fade into the background when you have so many talents and skills to share?

There will always be those who will dislike you for whatever reason, don't let that distract you, not everyone is going to support your goals, there will be those who will doubt your capabilities or measure your skill set on academic achievements, this is their own limiting beliefs at play and nothing to do with you. Ultimately there will be those who simply will not believe that your dreams are even viable, they will gossip behind your back about your foolish ways, they will indulge their own egos, preaching from the podium about all your faults while completely oblivious to their own.

You can step out from underneath all of this, overcoming any fear in your life, striving for your ambition and silencing the doubters that you met along the way. Remember fear is a temporary thing that with enough self-belief can be overcome; regret on the other hand lasts forever. Once you understand your reservations and conquer your demons you will realise on reflection that the only thing that frightened you was created inside your own mind. Just imagine what your life might look like if you weren't afraid to try. Everything passes and is gone, even the most trying of situations. Take one day at a time; placing one foot in front of the other, if you are moving forward in the direction of growth, this too shall pass.

Quote

"Want to be the person that sets the standards for the changes you wish to see? Lead from the front and make it your life's work to inspire."

Geraldine Mair

Affirmation

I am a leader for change, I will not let my own thoughts hold me back, I will try new things and grab all the excitement that comes along with those experiences. I am inspirational. I will find the solution in every challenge and nothing will ever defeat me. I embrace my uniqueness.

Strategy

If anything terrifies you at the very thought of it, decide in that moment that you want a solution more than you are afraid of taking the steps to fix it.

1. Keep track of your own thoughts; listen to what they are saying to you. You can find ways to talk yourself out of anything that worries you or initiates change. Your fear is in your mind not in your reality.
2. Stop giving all your energy to anything that makes you feel paralysed or keeps you stuck.
3. Don't listen to people who criticise or rebuke you for being different or for having an idea that you are trying to pursue. They don't know how strong you really are.
4. Fear has the potential to kill dreams if you let it, but if you view any failure as nothing more than an opportunity to find another way, you will have learned the lesson and mastered your life.
5. Stop trying to fit in when you were born to stand out, embrace who you are and show it to the world with pride, you are miraculous.

81. Hurdles on Your Life Path

When you find yourself in the midst of a struggle, remember that it is not life opposing you; this is a sign that you are being re-directed. It is really important at this point you don't view what you see as your enemy but simply more of an opportunity and a chance to choose a different path.

Looking back on these times, you often see it was more like a best friend that moulded you into the person you are today, something that sent you on a detour and helped to navigate your way around the stumbling block.

It is now that you should remember to say thank you and trust that what has happened has given you a different viewpoint and more often than not a better outcome. All things that push or pull you strengthen your tenacity with each one that you undergo, some are more difficult than others and some can test your very resolve, but growth is often achieved by how much you are willing to mature with each test.

If you could sail through life with no worries, issues or problems you would have no capacity to deal with very much if it ever occurred, you wouldn't be equipped to surmount that peak, and there would be no growth towards the person that you are today. If there were never any hurdles how would you develop the competence to jump through the hoops? Blessings come in many disguises even if you resist seeing it at the time.

There are some who have faced the most painful tests, but one way or another they managed to utilise their experience and turn it into something positive. It can often take a whole lifetime to decipher the lessons but when you have the chance to amend the direction of your future, strive for the opportunity through the adversity. In reflection it can become the best lessons you will ever have had to learn. So, persevere in the midst of all you might face for it will become your definitive success.

Choose to Climb.

Quote

"Obstacles in life are just an opportunity to make you the strongest version of yourself through the completion of the climb, the true nature of a champion is the one who triumphs in spite of it."

Geraldine Mair

Affirmation

I am a problem solver; I am constantly learning how to face up to trials in my life. I view each one as an opportunity to learn and grow into the person that I strive to become. Nothing will stop me from getting things done.

Strategy

I suspect that every single day there will be issues or events that will demand a solution, whether it is at work, with a colleague, with the family, a relationship problem or something else. There are many small things every day that you have to try to sort through and move forward from.

1. Whenever there are larger issues at play like loss, grief or redundancy, find strength through relevant support groups, this helps towards development and a plan for action and solution.
2. Focus on the solution and never on the problem.
3. Nothing can be solved with the mind that created it, so you will need to develop a different approach to find the answers that you seek.
4. In life catastrophes and problems may be inevitable but they exist so therefore so does the solution to overcome it. When you have the awareness to anticipate this nothing will be too large for you to scale.

82. Finding the Courage to Move On

You are all very unique with different stories that have moulded your lives over the years, yet you all struggle with internal paradigms that cause you to lose belief in yourself. There are times in life that you may feel alone, isolated and separate from others; this can make you feel very vulnerable, powerless and alone.

Each day brings another chance, a clean slate, creating a blank page to change your story. How do you work through a painful feeling and expand it into growth? Is there a way that you could re-assess a particular situation in your life where you felt scared to take a risk, ask yourself this question: what will I lose if I don't change? But more importantly what can I gain by embracing it? Guilt and shame for a particular event traps you in self-defeating cycles, leaving you feeling powerless to change your life's conditions. Allowing yourself to air pain and feel the release can assist the clearing of the water; the alternative is that you muddy it further by keeping it all inside.

Internalising worry has the potential to affect all of your body systems. Your ability to control those responses becomes compromised and can transpire into unease or melancholy or both, placing you into a state of mental and physical imbalance. When you are in a continuous cycle of fight or flight, you risk this becoming your normal state, leaving you susceptible to illness further down the line.

If you feel unwell with the pressures of life it's your body alerting you to the internal discord you are placing it under, this then becomes the net you get caught up in and it starts a sequence that continues until you find a way to release it. Relaxation, meditation, talking therapies, massage and exercise all contribute to the production of healthy reactions in the body, helping to heal these physical indicators so the balance can return. So when a crisis strikes you are armed and ready to deal with it in the best way possible. Love yourself enough and let go.

Quote

"Be courageous enough to know that you are equipped to face anything in this life, you were made with a power that can never be replicated by anything else."

Geraldine Mair

Affirmation

I look after myself; I know the benefits of getting outside everyday in nature. I will spend time everyday readdressing my internal balance. I feel alive and happy. I am willing to let anything from my past go so that I can move forward in anticipation of the best.

Strategy

There are scientific studies being undertaken that correlate stress to the impact it has on life. There is overwhelming evidence that suggests some lifestyles are responsible for creating havoc with our health, emotionally, mentally and physically.

1. Invest time out for you; know that this is not an indulgence but the best way to care for your wellbeing. When you disconnect just for a few hours and engage in something that brings joy or relaxes you fully, a happier state of being is realised and in turn you are more capable of dealing with problems.
2. Look into meditation either on your own or through a practitioner that can guide you for the best results.
3. Take the time to invest into exercise and enjoy the fresh air, you don't have to pump weights for hours in a gym, walking for at least 30 minutes a day can have a fantastic effect on your health and your heart. It's amazing the clarity that comes when you remove yourself from the problems for a little while. Often with a clearer head this is when the solution can be found.

83. Following Your Inner Voice

Your conscience keeps you on the right path, and you will never be able to escape what your heart is telling you, so it would be better to listen to what they both have to say. Fear is nothing more than false expectations appearing real and these originate inside your own thoughts, love is the greatest power and can remove any doubt, it always wins through in the end in everything, if there is hate, anger, bitterness or fear it is simply from a lack of love for a situation or person.

You cannot be responsible for others, but you can refuse to participate in situations that feel wrong. There is energy in this space that is emitted from the person, event or group, you will have all witnessed this at some time, but sadly all too often you will place yourself into a position where you think you ought to just stick it out, even if it makes you feel very uncomfortable to do so.

When you find yourself in a situation that is distressing to you, excuse yourself and leave. There is no benefit hanging around those that are sapping your energy and replacing it with nothing but toxic sludge.

Not everyone will understand your journey or want to go with you; it's not yet the right time for them to do so. Don't judge them or their decisions listen to your own principles and follow that instead, when you live with authenticity you allow the right people to enter your life, the ones whose values resonate with your own.

You do yourself a massive disservice when you compromise everything that you are because you refuse to listen to what your own voice is telling you. There are people who will sacrifice their whole lives in the pursuit of popularity but the cost can be immense to the individual who takes this path. When you are committed to a life without limits you will never feel restricted or oppressed by someone else's opinion of you, so always *Choose to Climb,* by following this creed you give yourself permission to soar.

Quote

"When the voices inside your own head become louder and more profound than those you are listening to on the outside you will have mastered your life."

Geraldine Mair

Affirmation

I am the designer of my own life. I follow my own values always. My beliefs are important to me; they make me who I am, I will continue to follow my intuition as I know it is my internal scope for my highest and best.

Strategy

Influence and the desire to fit in while wanting to impress are very powerful vehicles that can keep you stuck in a vicious cycle, where it becomes very hard to grow beyond your reality. You might have a full circle of so called friends in your life but when you take the time to analyse their behaviours how much are they enriching your experiences.

1. When you spend all your time with people that are negative, judgemental and toxic you run the very real risk of becoming one of them.
2. When you run with the wrong crowd you will never get further than the crowd.
3. Be brave enough to step away from the masses, and you will see opportunities that were always there but because you had blinkers on due to others opinions, you became unable to see what was under your nose the whole time. Your potential is now limitless.
4. Step Out and Step Up into your new future.

84. Loving Your Life

When you get out of bed on Monday morning are you excited for the day, or are you one of those people that think "oh no, another week in a job I can see far enough"? Too many of you get up every day to go to a place of employment that fills you with dread and the only reason you are turning up is to collect a wage; internal conditioning, limiting beliefs and a fear of something different serve to convince you there is nothing better. You persuade yourself its best to stay with what you know and so decide to continue down the same path week in and week out. This sounds like the best description for insanity I have come across yet.

Try setting a goal for yourself if you're unhappy, refuse to accept that this is your life, you're the only person capable of changing it so take control and shake yourself up a bit, this is the only way doors can open where they were once closed, if you can find the courage to embrace change you will find your bliss once more.

Update your CV's, test the water, and be prepared to be rejected but don't give up. I have seen many people settle for a life that was less than they deserve, due to limited thinking. You get one shot at this so do what makes you happy, do what ignites the fire that is in you, when you find it Mondays are exciting not dreadful.

I found the answer in my own life by taking the time out to retrain in a completely different field of study, and it has created many opportunities since I made the decision to do so and given me a new perspective that I may have missed if I hadn't taken the chance.

I was full of fear not knowing what might transpire, but I was exhilarated at the same time and I choose to harness that energy instead and it guaranteed my own personal success. Waste no more time engaging in conversations about how you wish things were different, "Seize the day," show how capable you are of everything you wish to achieve. Welcome every morning with gratitude for the day ahead and see what it brings.

Quote

"You don't live once you only die once, so make the time you are gifted to spend on this wonderful earth a magical experience every day, remembering it's an amazing privilege."

Geraldine Mair

Affirmation

I love my life, I am grateful for all the miracles that are in my life, I am open to all that the universe is sending me today. I will no longer continue to participate in repetitive behaviour that stunts my growth. Today I will take massive action to change anything that is marring my days.

Strategy

Never accept a career that fills you with dread and saps you of your joy. Why would you choose to do this, never fall into the trap that you should just be grateful to have a job? Of course, it's a blessing to be employed, but if you are miserable at least start a process and get into action to change the status quo and look for a future that serves you better.

1. You will never know what you are missing if you never take a risk or look for an alternative.
2. There is always something better when you are open to it; many of you have transferable skills that could massively enhance another organisation.
3. Don't sell yourself short, or listen to your colleagues talking you out of anything different from what you know.
4. Change can be hard and a little scary when you are settled but joy is something that you should not be prepared to compromise for any fee.
5. Leaving undiscovered potential on the table only harvests regrets further down the line. Go for it!

85. Appreciating True Love

When you're in a committed relationship you must be prepared to invest the necessary time and attention into the growth of that union, complacency is the biggest destroyer of partnerships, when you stop paying attention or giving the time to the person you promised to share your life with then do you really deserve to have that man or woman.

When there is trouble in the relationship and you start to look for imperfection within each other you set the stage and a platform that erodes all the good that was once there. When faults become the only things that you see and spending quality time becomes less and less your run the risk of separation, divorce, affairs and a distance that can become so wide it is difficult to bridge the gap. There are a lot of relationships that can be repaired and brought back from the brink, but there has to be two willing parties ready to invest their all, when there is still love present all things are possible.

In your relationships always continue to look for the qualities that were there in the beginning and encourage the growth of those. A committed partner should always be able to see how beautiful you are, someone that is proud to walk beside you even when you're not looking your best, someone who takes care of you when you're scared or ill, kisses you when you make mistakes and loves you in-spite of it anyway. All great relationships are built on equal respect for each other and a willingness to forgive when either of you trip up.

Love fully, forgive completely and know that in our human-ness you are all flawed, don't search for perfection as this is a standard that no one will ever be able to honour.

It is so simple to forget to remember how important our special people are when you let life get in the way. You should never be too busy to recognise when your partner is feeling neglected, it's your job alone to cherish that person and never to leave them questioning your loyalty or love.

Quote

"Love is a blessing that not everyone gets the opportunity to discover, if it finds you hold on with both hands; it's an amazing feeling that can last a lifetime if you let it."

Geraldine Mair

Affirmation

I love and forgive, choosing to nurture my relationship with passion every day makes it much more likely to succeed. I give time freely and will refuse to make other tasks a priority when I know my attention needs to be put in the direction of my partner.

Strategy

We can all be guilty of getting caught up with our responsibilities but make the effort to have some special quiet time every week or month.

1. Share special time in each other's company without the usual distractions, if you have children it is even more important as life is so busy with little ones, but children need parents that love one another and are witness to that exchange on a regular basis.
2. Teach through your behaviour it's how your family will grow and form their connections later in life.
3. If you wish to gain a return into the investment that you made several years down the line then you will need to be prepared to try and make your partner a priority.
4. When you feel loved, valued and appreciated it makes you want to spend much more time together, it's the gift that just keeps on giving, creating a foundation that little can penetrate, encouraging an unshakable bond that can last a lifetime.

86. Accepting You're Special

You must not rely or look to others for your self-worth. The only person that can be responsible for that is you. If you find it hard to respect yourself or love all that you are other people will be unable to see it either.

Deciding to accept who you are completely can be so tough for some of you, you appear to be hard wired to see all the flaws and you listen to the voices of others who hold opinions about you that are untrue. Uniqueness is not a special quality that is only for the chosen few; it is in all of you. Each one has their own set of talents, little quirks, and a certain way of doing things; it's what makes you special giving you individuality and identity.

Be bold and be proud of who you are, never shrink in the shadow of another to make them feel more comfortable or to make yourself feel better in their company. There is nothing in this world that can raise another person to a higher place than the compliments from a genuine heart; it's of more value than money, status or class. You can be all that you were meant to be in this life, the very creation of a human being is a miracle of science in and of itself, yet you forget all the synchronicities that have happened for each one of you to be here at this very moment in time. The beauty lies in your individuality not in becoming a carbon copy of someone else.

If you feel there are elements about your personality, your character or your appearance that you want to change or improve, do it for yourself in order to show the world the best version of you, this is one of your most admirable qualities because you made the time to develop and grow and not because you thought someone else wanted you to. No one can make you feel less that you are; only you can do that. The fact that you breathe every moment without giving it a thought is such a miraculous thing. Be proud, take off the mask and show the world all you really are. *Magnificent.*

Quote

"If you're looking for something to prove how amazing you are, then look no further that the reflection that looks back at you, it's there for you to see, in every facet of your being."

Geraldine Mair

Affirmation

I am a gift to this world. I am a miracle. I know I am a special, I will be grateful for who I am and strive to improve that each day. My uniqueness is my greatest asset.

Strategy

You can only ever love others to the degree that you are competent of loving and accepting yourself, believing that you are capable of being loved and that you deserve that gift in your life.

1. Do the work on personal growth that is necessary for you to accept what is already true, if others have told you that you're not good enough or that you will never amount to anything it can easily penetrate your subconscious mind and rapidly become your truth.
2. Working on your beliefs needs to become a priority in your life, tell yourself everyday that this is not your truth and no one can tell you that it is.
3. Move away from anything or anyone that makes you feel less and get around those who lift you higher. You get to decide, you get to choose, and you always have that choice.
4. You cannot change the opinions of others, it's none of your business but you can certainly silence their voices by choosing to listen to your own, louder, stronger one instead.

87. Inner Strength

When challenges in life are becoming too much to bear and you have reached your limit, you can become desperate until you are in the grip of hopelessness. Finding yourself in a state of inertia is a terrifying position to be in, stuck in a limbo that has no way out can be completely suffocating.

When you find yourself in this dark place you are often unable to think of a solution to the problem or hurdle you may be facing. Taking time out, however little can calm the nerves, rest the mind and the body, giving clarity to your perspective, it can help you to evaluate your principles and the reasons you react so strongly to certain things.

You only allow external events to affect you when you give them authorisation to take hold; there is an untapped reserve that lies dormant inside each one of you so give it your permission to emerge when you are tested.

There are no magic wands and no one to do the internal work for you, but I know a person that can show you how to overcome anything, that person resides inside of yourself. It can show you how to keep moving forward in the face of any misfortune, if you dig down far enough you will find that Inner Strength. When you take the time to care for yourself and harness your power it becomes an act of endurance and not any kind of self-indulgence. It is in fact necessary to help you to cope with the problems you will inevitably face over the course of your life.

Many things that test your tenacity can be overcome, for you are all equipped to do so, and when you are overwhelmed know that reserve tank is there and you can harness it to your advantage and withdraw that power. Remember to get up more times than life pushes you over and you will never be defeated, when you take the time to reflect on what has challenged you or brought you pain, it becomes apparent that your inner strength to defeat it is now reinforced for it was there all along.

Quote

"All of our greatest accomplishments in this life always happen from the inside that is where our maximum strength lies."

Geraldine Mair

Affirmation

I am strong enough to triumph over any challenge that I am faced with throughout the course of my journey. I have been blessed with the power of faith, giving me always the choice to rise. I am a force for good.

Strategy

There is only ever one person that can take you beyond any prison that you place yourself into. You are the ones who are completely responsible for the circumstances you allow into your experience and therefore you are the only ones that can alter that status to something that serves you better.

1. You can always get help from professionals that can show you a better standpoint and I encourage you to do so if you feel the task is insurmountable. But remember you are the one that will always have to do the work to change your outlook on any situation or problem.
2. Nothing can defeat you when you take away its power to do so, regardless of your age you will have already endured and defeated many challenges of differing degrees, the realisation of this proves how resilient you are.
3. Tap into your internal power that is always there, when you change your mind about a situation that you are facing the outlook ultimately changes to match your feelings.
4. Harness your inner strength to look at it from a different vantage point and get the necessary help to be able to move beyond the hurdle, where it becomes nothing more than a memory you will have learned a valuable lesson.

88. Finding Your Purpose

When you seek your purpose for life and the reasons you are here, your heart is your best tool to access your true purpose and passion. Ask yourself what brings you the most joy? When you search your soul for the answers to this question it can take time, and it will be challenging as most of you will have never explored this side of yourself, or you don't really have a clue. When you become inspired, excited and driven to excel in something, this is your spirit expressing itself, when you take your head out of the equation and lead from your heart, you naturally become more content and motivated to explore all the possibilities.

Your story is an important one and you were put here to have an impact on others no matter how small, everyone wants to feel significant because it's a basic human need, when you try more things it ignites new possibilities in each one of us that may have been dormant before. Finding something that stirs those emotions can sometimes take a lifetime to find, but it's not a race it's a journey that helps you to expand and rediscover elements that you may have missed. With a new understanding it opens the likelihood of a chance to see many things you may never have thought about. It doesn't matter how old or how young you are, when you become aware and act nothing can be withheld from you if you are prepared to take everything you experience on your journey as a teacher.

It's easy to stay where you feel comfortable but it's exciting when you push yourself and you introduce an element of uncertainty into the mix. Sometimes when you do things at a moment's notice that's when you have your biggest breakthroughs and this can drive your life in a totally different direction. So, stop thinking that there is only one purpose for your life for there can be many. Choosing to focus on that illusive Holy Grail can leave a feeling of failure or wasted time in the pursuit of happiness that you didn't find. Embrace the idea that your purpose is to love life fully, jump in and try new things; engage in unknown experiences yet to be discovered, in doing so you allow your inner desires to be realised and with it a whole new course for your life.

Quote

"The reason you can't find your purpose is because it's not lost... Follow what you feel a natural passion toward doing in your career or hobby and you'll discover a wonderful fulfilment through an evolving sense of purpose along the journey."

Derek Mair

Affirmation

I will participate in new and exciting experiences and by doing so I open myself up to potential that may not yet have been realised. I will live my life by design and do what fills me with joy. Happiness is my birth right.

Strategy

Why do you continue to spend so much time, sometimes years even, in situations that drain you of your bliss, is it because you are fearful of change? Is it because you don't feel that you deserve or are entitled to anything better?

1. Do not allow yourself to be conditioned to settle for your lot in life?
2. Habitual beliefs can penetrate the very depths of your mind becoming your truth, work on your internal paradigms and replace them each day with new thoughts that allow you to feel deserving of any outcome that you are chasing.
3. Stop making excuses; if you dislike your career start today to take the necessary steps to change the direction of your journey.
4. Learn new things, gain additional skills, send out CV's to potential employers, if you are interested you will come up with every excuse as to why you can't, but when you are committed to a process there isn't any force out there that can prevent you from changing your life.
5. Do it *NOW!*

89. Sharing Your Gifts

The way that you make others feel every single day is the most valuable currency you possess; all that you obtain in this life that is material will eventually crumble and fall apart. In the end all that will be left of you and your gifts is what was in your heart.

You are a light shining through the darkness, your very essence as an individual cannot be replicated by any other, your inimitability is the greatest part of who you are, out of over seven billion people on this planet there will never be another person that is just like you, isn't that the most amazing miracle when you really think about it. You are so much more than a creation; you are in fact a masterpiece.

There are so many people that I have come across during my own life's journey that are so frightened to ask for anything more that life has given them, perhaps out of fearfulness or unworthiness that they never aim for it. When you invest your time to discover, expand and contribute to those gifts it becomes a spiritual exercise. There can only ever be two motivation factors in this life that encourage us to be more or cause us to be less. These are love and fear.

You're gifts and talents are never meant to be hidden, they were given to you for sharing them with the world, allow all that is in you to blossom like a beautiful flower for people will remember how you made them feel. There is no more room for those that wish to hide in the back playing small, this is the time for you to step out from beyond the veil and start leading. Share all that you are in a big way and let's start celebrating that instead. There are always choices to be made, but decide in this moment to only choose love, love for life, love for the possibilities, and love for the opportunities... *Choose to Climb*.

Quote

"Choose to climb in this life; reach for the summit that awaits you with all of its wonder. It's your duty to do so every single day."

Geraldine Mair

Affirmation

I am talented. I am gifted. I am a masterpiece. I choose to acknowledge my gifts and skills that were given to me in the beginning and I will continue to improve myself with every action I take, it is my choice and I choose to give back to others that which has been placed in my care.

Strategy

There are so many times in this life that I have come across those people who shy away from expressing their god given talents, they don't want to come across as brash, full of themselves or egotistical. They want to fit in they want to be accepted so they choose to dim their light so that they don't offend others.

1. You are here to expand, to grow and to share, you are not here to hide, cover up or get by, if you are in the company of people that you hide your authentic self from, the only thing that needs to change is the company you are keeping.
2. Step away from anything that suppresses those gifts and start using them so that everyone can appreciate your talents.
3. Opportunities can only find you if you are willing to audition.
4. There will be some people over the course of your story that won't be able to go to the next chapter, don't be sad, they're not meant to be there, let them go and step into your own light and shine like the star you were born to be. The people who are meant to be in your life will come onto your path at the right time and be your biggest fans.

90. Finding Compassion for Others

Compassion is a feeling that moves you, one that enables care for others who are going through difficult times. It is called kindness because it elicits the good in others and embraces the distressed. When you can articulate feelings in yourself that cause you to move from judgement to caring, then understanding another's pain lets you embrace true empathy.

This creates a shift from isolation to connection; a real feeling of trust is generated and expressed. It's much like any other skill that can be taught, learned and expanded upon with practice. There are enormous amounts of benefits from choosing to use this approach. When you learn to have compassion for another's suffering it leads to an increase in the DHEA hormone that fights and counteracts the aging process while reducing your levels of stress responses in your body. It engages brain altering functions to allow the individual to feel a real sense of contribution to another in a positive way, which in due course lifts that human being also.

When people are hurting it can cause them to hurt others due to an inability to channel that pain in a positive way. It's a natural human response to react to anyone who offends one of your own values and this creates a reaction that is often marred with contempt or anger. Everyone is fighting battles and it's important to see the individual behind the mask and find what the core issue really is, it can be challenging but it can be rewarding when you learn how to diffuse a heated situation when you understand that there may be something else at play. Meet anger with sympathy, cruelty with a kind word and frowns with a smile. When you take the time to break down the walls that others have built so high it prevents anyone from getting through you have learned how to be truly compassionate to the wounds that live within them. When you meet any kind of discord with a calm loving approach you are opening a level playing field and a platform for solution and trust. Let's all try to be a little more understanding of the challenges that many face on a day-to-day basis and make it your purpose to help them out from beneath it.

Quote

"There will only ever be one weapon that we will need in the future to overcome all the hurt in this world, that weapon is love."

Geraldine Mair

Affirmation

I replace any anger or discord for others with compassion; everyone has a different view of this world and expresses themselves accordingly. I will lead through changing my approach first, I will try not to condone what I don't understand and always try to listen more that I speak.

Strategy

There will be times in life that you will meet people who will make you uncomfortable due their behavioural patterns or the way they treat or speak to others. When a person loses someone that they love it is obvious where the pain has originated and so it can be easier to show support. However, when it is not so obvious and the pain in a person has developed over time it can be easy to come from a position of judgement or hoping that karma pays them a visit as some kind of punishment.

1. Most people that come from this platform are very wounded indeed from circumstances that you will know nothing about.
2. It's better to be kind than to be right.
3. Be prepared to be gentle even when another is throwing fire onto your path, a compassionate response can help to bring about trust again so that individual realises in that moment not everyone is out to hurt them.
4. It's a skill that can be learned but the most valuable one that you can ever invest the time in perfecting.

91. Believe in the Best Today

I hear a lot of stories about people waiting until they are ready to embark on a dream or a purpose that they have for their life. I feel this is such a tragedy. Waiting for the right opportunity, more money, the exact environment or the right people only creates the perfect conditions for a sink hole to develop, one that will swallow you whole.

There will never be the right time because there will always be a reason for you to find obstacles that make the situation less than perfect, here's the thing, your ducks will never all be in a row, there is no such thing, you need to learn to jump and grow your wings on the way down.

There is no promise of tomorrow and all your yesterdays have gone, the only time you must really affect is *NOW!* Don't waste another moment in analysis of your life; take whatever action is necessary to push you beyond your restrictions and into something better. If you are unhappy where you are, unfulfilled at work or a relationship, make this your day to alter the trajectory of that path.

There is only one thing that stops you from reaching your highest and best and that's the nonsense that you keep telling yourself every single day. The self-talk that resides inside of your own head and creates all the negative responses or, those you spend too much time with that encourage you to find reasons why you shouldn't; this only adds additional weight to belief patterns that restrict your movement further.

You can follow your dreams, when you realise that *YOU* make the decisions for your future, no one else has any power over you unless you pass them the baton and the responsibility for your destiny. You deserve as much happiness as anyone else; you only have one life but are given as many chances as you need to get it right. Follow your heart and your joy will surely follow.

Quote

"The beauty of each new day that is born after every sunrise is an opportunity to try again and to believe in the best day yet."

Geraldine Mair

Affirmation

I choose to believe that my best days are out in front of me; I am continually growing into the best version of me. I am open to the abundance of the universe.

Strategy

The only way to change your life is to take full responsibility for all of it. Once you embrace the concept that your reality is nothing more than a reflection of your internal beliefs and thoughts you can put the wheels in action to change the direction of any situation.

1. If you dislike something change it!
2. If you are complaining constantly stop it!
3. If you feel envious of others who have more than you, use this energy to your advantage instead of to your detriment, let it become the catalyst that drives you forward so that you too can have the life that you dream of and not just as an observer.
4. There is no one smarter that you, more talented than you or luckier than you, this is your internal talk that keeps you exactly where you are enduring the merry go round of your uneventful life.
5. Choose to believe in the best every single day, take steps to remove any negative influences that keep you stuck in an ongoing cycle.
6. Get around groups of people who run motivational workshops in your area or educate yourself everyday with material that allows you to view your live differently. Opportunities are everywhere when you are open to see them. You're in charge take control and be the change.

92. Understanding the Power of Love

Love *IS* power, it is without a doubt the most powerful feeling on the planet, nothing can come close to the exhilaration that can be felt when you know that you are loved. Love is the strongest power there is. No one can clarify why they love a person; it's an intangible thing, an internal feeling that is more real than anything you can explain. It's a heart that skips a beat when you see your love, it's a moment of pride when watching your child achieve something wonderful, it's seeing their face at the end of a difficult day, and it's a strong embrace that makes you feel safe. When you understand the real force that is present in this very powerful emotion and decide to jump into the passion that will inevitably follow, you will know what the power of love truly feels like for you.

Place no limitation on your life, even if you have been hurt in the past, when you are ready to embrace a partnership that is full and equal in all its parts then you will be able to bring all that you have into that union. If you are constantly making excuses as to why you cannot or will not love again, spend time working on your own beliefs, ask yourself what you are really frightened of by making the jump. There is always an element of risk when you enter into an agreement to make a life with someone else and there are times when it doesn't work as you had hoped it might have. But never close the door on love and never tar those you meet with the same untrusting brush that may have kept you in the single camp up till now, loneliness is a painful concept that becomes much more apparent with age, you are meant to be with others, sharing your lives and building memories.

Experience makes us stronger and allows us the option of selecting a better match, choosing a little wiser every time until you meet that soul who makes you feel complete and loved for exactly who you are, with no need for alterations of any kind. Love is the universal language of the world requiring no words to provide understanding. When your soul drive is towards another person's happiness that is essential to your own, you will have found that unmistakable bond you have been searching for.

Quote

"When we emit love out into the world it inevitably draws the same back and a life with no limits will surely follow."

Geraldine Mair

Affirmation

I feel love for all that I have. I am open to receiving all the love that is in the universe. Love is all around me in nature, in people, in partnerships, in children and families and I choose to become a part of it all.

Strategy

Love attracts, fear repels.

1. Embrace any opportunity that gives you the chance to show that love to the world. Helping another person, loving your family, being a good supportive friend or work colleague, make love your goal every single day that you are here, harness the power that comes with the understanding of this influence and teach others through your own example.
2. You can have impact in others' lives and you can change any situation with a different response.
3. If you are ever in doubt with any situation in your life that you are finding challenging, love is the answer as it is generally down to a lack of love that creates the friction in the first place.
4. Choose to elicit the power of love it resides inside of you, set it free.

93. Do Not Entertain Negative Energy

Are you guilty of throwing negative energy at others with the intention of offending? If you are, then realise you are interfering with their self-esteem and self-worth, you have created the potential to affect their perception of themselves and their environment.

When you engage with this kind of behaviour you are pushing a lot of harmful vibration out into the universe that has nowhere to go except right back to the person that it came from. What you give out is what you get back. Energy has a magnetic power all of its own and the potential to hurt or harm another by its very nature, think before you speak because your words can wound deeper than any blade.

When you find a constructive way of dealing with issues then solutions can be found that prevent any detrimental responses. Everyone is imperfect by human nature and therefore all capable of causing offence, when you give too much focus and attention to negative things you allow it to have more power and you become a beacon for disaster to court you.

Respect yourself by respecting others, realise that you are creating the drama by the very behavioural patterns that you are emitting. There can be no improvement until you realise that the change must start from within. Negative attitudes can only create negative responses it can be no other way it's the law of the universe.

Positive people attract all the good into their life not by luck or chance but on purpose, what goes on inside your own head will give you back the sum of what you're giving out to others. There is good news though for those willing to alter direction. You only have to be prepared to change your mind; in doing so a chain reaction occurs inside you that amends your thought patterns, when this takes place the rest will follow.

Quote

"Negativity drains, Positivity lifts, be very careful what camp you choose to pitch your tent in, it has the potential to raise you higher or infect your life with misery."

Geraldine Mair

Affirmation

I am a positive force. I am uplifting and responsible. I forgive those who have hurt me. I know that a change of mind can be the best decision for a different course to take root in my life. Today I will start working on a better more positive outlook for myself, knowing that in doing so I greatly increase my chances for a far better destination that the one I am currently on.

Strategy

It can be easy to be convinced or swayed to enter into a situation that you are less than comfortable, especially if you seek acceptance or friendship.

1. Never compromise your own values when your intuition tells you that it feels wrong, in my experience it's usually the correct response and you should listen to your own internal dialogue.
2. Negativity can never make you feel good about yourself or anything that it is attached to; only a positive approach to life and those who we choose to share it with can have real influence over our future in a constructive way.
3. Become conscientiously aware of the energy that you bring into every situation for it is your responsibility.
4. Protect yourself from the contamination that negativity brings and limit the time you spend with those who indulge in this emotion.

94. Selfish Versus Selfless

When you decide to help others though selfless acts you are choosing to enhance the quality of their life, but unconsciously you are improving your own in the process. The real joys in life are to be found in giving to others, not in what you are getting. So often you make the grave mistake of thinking it's the other way around. Life is just better in realising the rewards are gained when you share what you are with someone else, in doing so the wheels of change are set in motion with the potential for real transformations to occur.

A selfish person is driven by their ego and they lose so much over the course of their life without even realising it, if the time comes where an irreparable offence has occurred on their part, there is a lack of empathy to make any kind of amends, this keeps a repeat cycle going sometimes many, many times. It's only when egos get in the way and your own pride is placed above everything else that complete focus and perspective is lost.

There is a fine line between these two characteristics. It's imperative not to let yourself be taken advantage of through your good nature, when you allow others to abuse your time or your kindness there is no balance, this precious commodity is no less important than another's so protect it, give yourself emotional permission to refuse certain errands if they impinge on your own family time too much or cause a negative effect in the relationship.

Being helpful is a beautiful quality and you need that in life, just remember not to let it become the norm. If all your efforts are only going one way it drains all your resources and free time in the process. It is important to reward yourself with your own space too, this allows you to unplug from the world for a little while encouraging a healthy demeanour and keeps you mentality fit. Be careful that you are not negating your own responsibilities as a partner or parent due to unrealistic demands of others. This can become the catalyst for fracture and separation if you do not place the most important things in your life above everything else.

Quote

"There is a balance in life between what you give to others and what you give to yourself, both are necessary for a content life."

Geraldine Mair

Affirmation

I value my time. I am giving. I understand the balance between giving and receiving both are valuable. I will invest the time required into myself to ensure my health mentally and physically are always at their best, this is an important part of self-care and important for my well-being.

Strategy

A selfless approach should always be one of balance where you grasp opportunities as they arise to be of assistance to another.

1. Never help anyone whose has a repetitive pattern of consistently draining your own resources.
2. Be ok with refusing to participate in the relentless demands of others when you realise that they are not respecting your boundaries.
3. People will treat you how you allow them to, so be mindful of how much you are giving away.
4. Take time to look after your own body and mind this is not selfish but necessary to operate at optimum levels.

95. Understanding Real Fulfilment

If you have to make an effort to be happy or exude a personality of the same, then chances are you are hiding from something and presenting a fake persona to others. Your happiness is an emotion it is not something that you acquire but rather something you are. When you enjoy each day, and live in the present moment this is the vehicle that creates the foundation for true fulfilment to thrive.

When you talk about wanting more happiness, your understanding of this emotion is often linked to material gains that are outside of yourself. For example, new cars, eating out, holidays abroad, amazing relationships, socialising with friends, being more popular, and so on. But these things contribute more to the feelings of pleasure and they are not long lasting, and although this is great, it's not the same as happiness. People confuse these two states. For example, if someone has a drug habit, they would have been pursuing pleasure to get to the ultimate state of euphoria, but because of its addictive nature will end up far from happy. When people chase the concept of immediate gratification it very rarely results in any kind of long-term satisfaction. Remember the special moments in your lives, not the things that you accumulated over the years that you changed whenever the fashions did.

Research has shown that the pursuit and focus of superficial pleasures and material aims, can lead to a more emotionally unstable, anxious and less happy individual over the longer term. Pleasure is the one thing that is advertised to us through various media every day of our lives but it is the shallowest in terms of satisfaction. Pleasure can become an additive giant, one that creates additional pressures in your life, especially if you are trying to create one that you have no means to support long term. Aim for a more concrete state of being instead, enjoying all the things that are already in your life that bring you immense joy. Pleasure in and of itself is not a bad thing but don't look for the fast fixes choose to share it with something or someone that is routed in real happiness the rewards are a great deal better, and last for much longer.

Quote

"Pleasure is generally a consequence of temporary action; fulfilment is a consequence of permanent passion."

Derek Mair

Affirmation

I am genuine, I am authentic, I am grateful for my life and everything that I have been blessed to have. I understand that my rewards will be better when invested in worthwhile activities that create lasting memories for me and others.

Strategy

You will never find what you seek if you continue to believe that the answer to this question resided outside of you. When you are looking to design a fulfilled life then be grateful for all that is already in your experience. This allows you to see opportunities to allow more to come into your reality.

1. Invest the time required to develop relationships, your passions and your family this will bring much more rewards than anything materialistic ever can. Spend all your energy in the pursuit of this goal.
2. Collect memories not things, they last much longer and have much more weight in reflection.
3. You will be much more likely to remember times in your lives that were magical or even tragic that you can recall in a heartbeat. In the end this is what you will commit to memory because of how it made you feel.

96. Knowing There is Always Hope

When you have courage, it will not always be the loudest roar in the room, sometimes it is nothing more than the little voice at the end of a difficult day that tells you to try again tomorrow. Even if you think you are the only person left who believes in you when you have hope, it will still be enough.

Your beliefs begin internally, you do not need to have a team of followers cheering you on from the side-lines; you do however need an inner conviction that reinforces how you feel about yourself.

When you're in a position that you feel cornered it's more important than ever to remain in a state of hope, in doing so you hold within you the power and ability to take the required action and make a difference. You will never get to where you want to go if you continue to berate yourself or go over all the reasons why you can't. In the light of day most things are rarely as bad as you thought they were and with renewed vigour you can set about finding solutions instead of building walls.

In the darkest of skies, it only takes just one star to pierce through the black space, when you are lost these tiny shards of light can come in many forms, a good friend, a loving relative, an inspiring mentor, and those special people already believe in your potential that is hiding just out of sight.

Everyone needs support in times of despair, it can help you to cope just knowing the safety net is there. Encouragement from others is the very foundation that helps you get back up after you have fallen, so never ever give up. There is a time and one true essential in life that keeps you moving forward, an expectation of hope that something in the future can change and bring you to a new place where you can build, once more a better tomorrow. That time is *NOW!*

Quote

"When there is hope for anything, there is potential for growth and through growth comes change and the ability to expect the best."

Geraldine Mair

Affirmation

I embrace change. I have courage in myself. I believe that there are no boundaries however bad it may seem, if I hold on to hope I have everything I need to overcome any difficulty.

Strategy

When you stop hoping for better you inevitably settle for existing instead of living. You were not born to survive, you are here to thrive and there is always hope in any situation or a solution to be found when you refuse to continually beat yourselves up when you mess up.

1. Become a person who champions cooperation, communication and collaboration, there is always a way out of anything, adding weight to the belief that hope in yourself and others achieves great things.
2. Never be beaten down by life and all the challenges that it will give you, surrounding yourself with a good support network creates the foundation for hope to thrive, if tragedy should strike at any point there will always be the loving support of a strong arm to help you through the worst.
3. Once your embrace hope you will hold within you the capacity to show empathy towards others in times of need.

97. The Power of You

Have you ever considered reading a few positive quotes before you go to bed at night instead of watching news that is generally full of negative zapping stories? Your thoughts are driven within your unconscious mind by the very things that you entertain, and it is even more evident before you turn in for the night because that is what your brain will process until you wake in the morning.

Positive thinking is like a powerful car with a great engine, it can take you anywhere even to the top of a steep hill, it is a catalyst that has the power to produce, energy, momentum, more initiative, and happiness, and an internal desire that can change your life direction and help find the answers you seek to the problems that hold you back.

You are blessed now with incredible power, it can take many years of personal experience good and bad for you to fully understand and appreciate what you are made of. Most of you do not give yourself enough credit when faced with pain or pressure, unable to realise you are equipped with a survival instinct to triumph over it. Your internal quality is in there and can take on every challenge that you face and find a solution to carry you over the hurdle and back onto the track.

Learn to train your mind to think in terms of "I can" or "it's possible", "I have the strength to get through this". If you close the curtains you will darken the room, but you can also open them and let in the light. It is always a matter of choice. Your mind is your room. Will you stay in the dark or step into your brilliance? There is an invisible force inside and if you harness it you can gradually change your mindset, transform your life, and attract good things to you. There is an untapped potential that you can all access, gaining ground in self-confidence can open you up to an inner strength that was already there but you were oblivious to see.

Quote

"There is an invisible power in each one of us that rises to the surface when needed, ready to take on any challenge."

Geraldine Mair

Affirmation

I am possible. I am a fighter. I am a champion and I can overcome trials easily in my life. I trust the solution to always come when I need it. I am capable and when I view everything as a teacher or a lesson I can embrace a new reality. I am worthy of this and I will it to power.

Strategy

When you are faced with a test in life or if you are in the process of trying to overcome an event or tragedy take strength from other experiences that you have managed to conquer in your past.

1. Don't believe your own hype, the power you have inside can be the guide to silence your internal critic.
2. When you find yourself reacting to an issue in an old way, you will get the same result until you become the pioneer of your habitual thoughts and break free from the sequence.
3. Positivity cultivates change; negativity keeps you fixed in disengaging patterns. You will learn over time that you are stronger than you ever believed and in reflection you will soon realise that this difficult chapter in your life will also pass and become a memory just like all the others.
4. You are a champion, a fighter and a survivor with the ability to survive any stumbling blocks.
5. Read the affirmation for this passage many times until it sinks deep into your unconscious allowing a new habit pattern to be formed that you can grow from in a positive way.

98. The Power of Anger

This is a paralyzing emotion, when you find yourself in this arena you can't get anything done. I have met people who think it's important, passionate, and an igniting emotion that makes them feel powerful. I don't think it's any of that, I believe it's helpless and weak and is in fact the absence of all control. When you give away your peace to another you give away any chance of resolve for a particular situation.

People who are angry are not easy to be around; they create a very awkward atmosphere and a negative environment that is difficult to feel any joy in. when you realise that there is an issue you must be prepared for change, this can be achieved when you decide to release any past fears that may still be lingering in your unconscious mind, that cause you to go to this emotion first when challenged.

When you fully engage your aggression, knowing the harm it can cause it creates hostility and notable ferocity towards others, it provides you with nothing that you can repair. Antagonism and rage are cemented deep in insecurity, causing conflict within that personality; they stem from an unresolved space inside that longs to be healed but has no knowledge as to how to make it so. It can be from a learned behaviour that they witnessed during childhood, a vehicle that was always used first to show power and control over the weak, cyclical in its origin it is what keeps repetitive patterns showing up in the present.

As individuals you have allowed that programming to take hold in your own consciousness and although uncomfortable for most, it can often be the only driver available for some to protect themselves from conflict or threats. I have discovered by observation in myself and in others that I have no use for it whatsoever. How you choose to react emotionally is a choice in any situation, there can be no winners or solutions when you approach from this angle, unless you are willing to drown in your own unpredictability refrain from holding onto anything that has the power to pull you under.

Quote

"The finest line is barely visible between love and hate, both are capable of enormous emotion, but only one brings harmony."

Geraldine Mair

Affirmation

I release past hurts that reside within, I forgive myself for any mistakes or damage that I caused along the way. I invest in me and from this moment forward I will consciously try when irritated to direct that energy in a positive way or remove myself until I am able to find composure again.

Strategy

If you are experiencing a real problem with control and it is affecting your close relationships please seek the relevant help from a therapist to identify your personal triggers so you can overcome this dreadful malady. You can all show elements of discord from time to time, but when this behavioural pattern becomes your personality you are entering onto very dangerous ground that has nowhere to go but down.

1. Invest time working on yourself this will help you come to terms with who you are and any situation that either brings you bliss or trips your switch.
2. Investigate the historical thoughts or feelings that you believe have created this reaction in you and act to fix it either personally or professionally.
3. Take up an interest that is solely for yourself that you enjoy. Finding expression this way can address dissonance in a positive way and help you to feel better about yourself.
4. Find ways of channelling your anger in a more constructive way that you can use for a positive outcome instead. Exercise can be great for this.

99. Success In Work

As you navigate your path through life be open to encouraging influence and support. In group environments you often fail to consider ideas from others that are frequently better than your own, you do this because unconsciously you feel that your position is threatened in some way. Why not make this the moment to change the way that you frame things?

If you meet others who challenge you please let them and get excited at the prospect of what they can bring into the process. Expanded awareness and a culture of inclusion support open forums where everyone gets to add their own ideas and therefore feel as if they have much more than just a job. When this status is reached you are no longer turning up for a wage, you have a real sense of contribution and a massive win, win, for all involved creating a spectacular environment to thrive in.

To succeed in anything, it is always an easier journey when it is something that motivates and inspires you. When you are excited it creates momentum and in turn a passion that is impossible to hide from others. Your appetite for growth and contribution can create the actions that deliver results; the eagerness you show for your work can become contagious around others, instilling them with inspiring to want to do the same.

Spending time with these kinds of people has the capacity to change your life. Everyone knows something that you don't. You can't know everything and it's a very narrow-minded individual who thinks they can, remember when you are willing to come from a position of constant improvement the sky is the limit. Always share all your knowledge and skills with others to encourage, and inspire, use what you learn to bridge the gaps; this creates the opportunity that allows everyone involved to connect to a brighter future.

Quote

"When we are true leaders, we illicit the greatness freely in those beneath us with the intention to raise them up to their maximum potential."

Geraldine Mair

Affirmation

I choose a career that fulfils me and unites with my values, I am continually learning to improve my prospects and I enjoy bringing my ideas to the table. I am willing to pass on all I know to benefit another. I constantly come from a platform of cooperation and never competition, as this is where everyone thrives as a group.

Strategy

If you are in a position of influence at work use this privilege well. Even if you are aspiring to improve your situation through promotion, you can start from wherever you are making changes as you go.

1. Never feel threatened by another individual; it is only a reflection of your own insecurities.
2. Growth comes from expansion and sharing with the whole, this is how everyone wins.
3. Invest in people for here is the true wealth in any organisation.
4. Lead from the front always and show those people around you that you have the capacity to learn from those above and beneath you.
5. When you have integrity and respect for your team they will support you because they trust your judgement, when this is achieved you will become a force to be reckoned with and an asset to any company.

100. Leaving a Memorable Legacy

During the journey of your life, people will remember the way that you touched their hearts, how you made them feel and the love that you shared with that exchange. When you wish to affect any space and you do so with a positive influence you can be sure it will lead to a much happier and content life. Bravery, compassion and generosity, are an inspiration and even more so when you have these role models in your own circles, they drive the change and encourage you to emulate their lead.

What a wonderful thought, knowing you hold within you the capacity to create ripples that help others to climb. You have the potential for all of this and it can begin within your own family.

Most of you at some point in your life will wish to be someone that others look up to or admire. One of these may well be at that very special time you bring a new life into the world and you possess the potential to influence a new generation.

When you give of yourself to those whom you love and care about two lives are automatically enriched because of the act. If you start with that intention the knock-on effect can be remarkable. Gratitude and joy as a foundation that you grow from will be reflected in all your actions and ultimately all those you love will become witness to that gift.

Legacies will always be the result of conscious actions ones that you weave into your life daily, imagine being the person that others reference with gratitude and because of the choices you made it left an unforgettable mark instead of a wound. No matter what turns up in life be good to people, this is what you will be measured by when you are absent, start to build all the parts of your personality that will outlive your physical presence, in doing so you inadvertently leave a inheritance that can help many others to follow your impeccable lead and hopefully they too will choose to climb.

Quote

"When your actions in this life create the foundations that inspire many to do more for others, then you have left a very important message in this world indeed."

Geraldine Mair

Affirmation

I know that I have the potential; no matter how small, to make a difference in the life of another, I will make it my goal to create something of influence that inspires others and lives on long after I have gone.

Strategy

This time you are living in now is your chance to bridge the gaps created by separation. You are born beautiful and full of wonder and inquisitiveness. Let's look at life once more through the lens that you came into this world with and leave a legacy of yourself that you can be proud of.

1. Write down the top five things that you feel are your best qualities and use them in every area of your life.
2. Do the same with the top five things that you feel you could develop or change into something that serves your goals better and then take the action necessary to alter that trajectory.
3. Start removing the negativity from your own experience replacing it with positive options instead.
4. Keep climbing until you are happy with the reflection that you see each day, knowing that you are making the changes you feel are needed to have a constructive impact on others that you engage with.
5. Leave a great impression of a person who has taken responsibility, and chosen to live with integrity always.

Final Thoughts

To all my wonderful readers, I have discovered over the course of my own life that there will be tough times that all of us will have to navigate, and everyone that you know will experience them to different degrees. This book can equip you with many strategies for a whole myriad of challenges you might come across on your journey.

Please reference it often, seek out the messages that inspire you to act and resolve the problem at hand. You cannot fix anything in life with the same approach that you created it with, so try a different way instead. In doing so you open the doors to potential and possibility for things to turn out far better than you originally hoped for.

In conclusion, I wish for each one of you that hold this volume in your hands, a real insightful glimpse of how approaching your life from an alternative viewpoint can have a crucial effect on your future. Start today, because with the smallest of changes the ability to transform even the most sceptical of minds becomes a possibility. Share it with your friends, families, colleagues or anyone you come across on your path that needs lifted.

My dream for this book would be for it to reach as many people as possible with the intention that it enhances their life experience in a positive and profound way leaving them with enormous benefit and value.

Treat it as your own personal journal, place notes in the columns and highlight sentences that strike a chord with you, mark your favourite passages that have had the biggest impact on your life and apply what you learn so that real transformation can take shape in your life towards a more positive direction.

It has been my greatest honour to be able to share with you my experience and knowledge gained over my lifetime and what others have freely shared with me during my time as a therapist.

Please take every opportunity to appreciate and love all that you are and all those who have or continue to enrich your life in wonderful ways. Enter every exchange with the intention of seeking the best outcome always, even when you are being tested. Make it your goal to increase your experiences while you are here and may you always present the best version of yourself to the world every day.

You are a miracle, you always have been; never let anyone dull your shine for you are illumination in motion. Your legacy will be the memories that you leave behind when you are no longer here. Make them amazing ones for memories last forever in the hearts of those whom you touch.

May your lives be full, happy and blessed.

With all my love Geraldine

Quote

"True visionaries are those who are never beaten by any problems; through inspired actions they always find the solutions they seek, whilst those who never search for answers will always be sinking in theirs."

Geraldine Mair

Acknowledgements

I am incredibly grateful to all the people that have helped me realise this dream and pulled everything together into this volume.

My unconditional love and gratitude goes out to my husband Derek, who put up with me during the writing of this book and for taking the time with a careful eye to read all that I have written, and our son for his constant encouragement and all our interesting talks many that were centred around the passages in this book, you are so inquisitive and interesting you just make me smile. You are my very own bright star in a dark sky and I am so proud of you.

A special thanks to Grosvenor House Publishing whose team of experienced professionals, have led me though the process every step of the way and understood exactly what I wanted to achieve and then set about making it so. Your amazing team have made this book possible and helped me to get it out into the world. It has been an absolute pleasure working with you and for all the skills that you possess to help authors like me I am forever indebted to you all.

To Tamsin Richardson owner of Good Day Studio. My graphic designer who listened to our vision on our video calls and brought back amazing illustrations of exactly what I depicted. She realised how important it was to me and my husband to create the brand Choose to Climb and her talents are evident. Thank you, lovely lady I wish you all the success in the world.

And finally, to all the people that will take the time to read what I have written, I hope that in doing so you will find the champion that is alive inside and you begin to design your own future from this point onwards and never have a desire to conform ever again. *Choose to Climb.*

About the Author

Geraldine Mair (Nicol) was born in the winter of 1968, raised in a working-class family and is the youngest of three children; all girls. She enjoyed a happy childhood with many friends and always showed a creative flair mainly through her artwork.

She attended the local primary and then high school where she left at 17 years of age. Most of her adult life has been spent in food retail where she had many happy years and fond memories of those whom she worked with. Married to Derek in the summer of 1990 and still happy and together today, they welcomed their only son into the family in June 1994 and he has been the light of their lives ever since.

After 25 years in the same career she decided to take her life in a very different direction, a desire to give back and help people became a driving force. So, when she turned 45 she invested her time learning how to become a fully qualified complimentary and holistic therapist. She then completed diplomas in additional areas to expand her knowledge and support her practice. She started a business as soon as she was trained from a converted treatment room in her home, where she now has a thriving business treating many clients every day, bringing her immense fulfilment.

After only a few months she recognised that many people she met had personal, professional or emotional challenges as we all do, so she started writing upbeat positive passages and posting them onto facebook in the hope that it would help those who were struggling in a constructive way. From here she started to receive private messages requesting that she write a book with motivational passages for people to keep. Embracing the challenge, she took it onboard and set to work, the completion of this goal was realised in the spring of 2017 and is now what you hold in your hands today.

Together with her husband the plans for *Choose to Climb* Seminars and Retreats are now being realised.